Financial Independence, Retire Early

Discover the Secret Path to Freedom, Wealth, and Free Life.

I Will Teach You to Become Rich Through Financial Investments and Real Estate.

Dan Graham & Matthew Buffet

Financial Independence, Retire Early
Dan Graham & Matthew Buffet

© Copyright 2020 by Dan Graham & Matthew Buffet. All rights reserved.

Disclaimer

In providing answers, neither Buffet nor Grahaam is acting as a certified financial planner or advisor or certified financial analyst and economist, CPA, account accountant, or lawyer.

Neither Buffet nor Grahaam makes any recommendations as to any specific securities or investments.

All content is for informational and general purposes only and does not constitute financial, accounting, or legal advice. You should consult your own tax, legal, and financial advisor regarding your particular situation. Neither Buffet nor Grahaam accepts any responsibility for any loss which may arise from accessing or relying on information in this book. And to the fullest extent permitted by law we exclude all liability for loss or damage, direct or indirect, arising from the use of this information.

This statement is legally binding as deemed by the Committee of Publishers Association and the American Bar Association for the territory of the United States. Other jurisdictions may apply their own legal statutes. Any reproduction, transmission, or copying of this material contained in this work without the copyright holder's express written consent shall be deemed a copyright violation as per the current legislation in force on the date of publishing and the subsequent time thereafter. The holder of this copyright may claim all additional works derived from this material.

Table of Contents

Table of Contents

Introduction

Who Is This Book for?

Disclaimer

What Is Financial Literacy?

What Is Financial Independence?

What Is Financial Freedom?

What Is Early Retirement?

What Will You Learn in This Book?

Chapter 1: Passive Income

What Is Passive Income?

What Is a Side Hustle?

The Importance of Passive Income for Retiring Early and Finding Financial Independence

Examples of Passive Income Streams and Their Earning Potential

E-Commerce?

Online Courses

Book Sales

Online Content Creation

A Note on Side Gigs and Earning Potential

How to Choose a Source of Passive Income

Passive Income Will Set You up for Investing Later on

How Passive Income Will Allow You to Retire Early

Chapter 2: Financial Literacy

The Benefits Of Financial Intelligence

Financial Terms and Information for Entrepreneurs or People With Side Hustles

Understanding Basic Financial Statements

Income Statements

Balance Sheets

Cash Flows

How to Ensure That Your Side Hustle/Business Is Making You Money, Not Costing You Money

How to Save the Most Money Possible

How to Use Goal Setting to Increase Chances of Success

How to Use This Income for Early Retirement

Chapter 3: Investment Funds

The Benefits of Investing

What Is Capital?

What Are Investment Funds?

The Benefits Of Investment Funds

Examples Of Investment Funds And How To Use Them To Make Money

ETF (Exchange-Traded Fund)

Low-Cost Funds

Stocks

Bonds

Commodities

401 (K)

TRF (Target-Risk Fund)

Mutual Funds

Hedge Funds

Where To Begin With Investing

Warren Buffet's Secrets

How to Avoid Making Bad Financial Decisions

Step 1: Identify your Spending Weaknesses

Step 2: Build a Financial Plan with Clear Goals

Step 3: Discipline Yourself Every Day

Step 4: Build Simple and Healthy Financial Habits.

Step 5: Change your Views of Money

Step 6: Create a Financial Backup Plan

Step 7: Reward Yourself When you've Achieved Financial Success

Step 8: Forgive your Mistakes and Move On.

Chapter 4: Real Estate Investments

What Are Real Estate Investments?

Examples Of Real Estate Investments

Commercial Properties

Event Space

Vacation Rentals

The Benefits Of Real Estate Investments

Types Of Properties

Rental Properties

House Flipping

Real Estate Investment Groups

Tips for The Negotiation Process

Which Properties Will Be Most Lucrative In the Long-Run?

Commercial Real Estate

Residential Rental Real Estate

Properties For Flipping

How To Find The Best Investment Properties

Using a Real-Estate Agent

Buying on your Own

Judicial Auctions

Finding Discounted Properties

How To Finance Your Property

Rent or Sell?

Other Options Related To Real Estate

Tips For Success

Chapter 5: Financial Tips For Success

Things to Keep in Mind When Starting Your Own Business

How to Be a Competent Money Manager

Chapter 6: Other Tips For Success

How to Make Investing a Habit

Work On Time Management

Persist, Persist, Persist!

Break Down Your Goals Into Smaller Pieces

Tips For Running a Successful Business

How To Keep Yourself On Track To Your Financial Goals

Pay Attention To Your Financial Mindset

Conclusion

Introduction

In our world today, we are bombarded with success stories of various entrepreneurs who started from nothing but are now easily making millions.

How did they get there?

What did they do that's different from the rest of us?

Although there is no clear-cut answer to this, significant research has shown that successful entrepreneurs have a specific combination of skills, the right mindset, and habits that make them successful.

In this book, I will share these secrets with you, and I will teach you the skills that you will need to develop and be as financially successful as you can be.

This book was written to help beginners become proficient in passive income techniques and strategies to achieve financial freedom and retire early!

If this sounds like what you are looking for, you are in the right place!

Who Is This Book for?

Not only is this book for beginners to the world of financial freedom and investing, but this book will help people who are more experienced to hone their skills and knowledge.

No matter what experience or knowledge you came with, this book will help you somehow, and you will be glad that you picked it up!

Note of Authors

Before we begin, we want to make something clear.

In the world of investments at any given moment in time, each reader could see very different results from one another with each person's specific set of technical skills and knowledge.

Furthermore, there is always a risk component involved in investing and trying to grow your wealth.

In the financial and entrepreneurial sphere, there are no mathematical certainties, only risk and reward.

It is up to each of you to decide which risks you are willing to take, and nobody can say for certain what the reward will be or whether there will be a reward at all.

This book is a source of general information, presented in a simple way, designed mainly for beginners who want to start understanding the rules of the game of wealth, and who want to be able to choose in an informed way the type of investment that best suits their personal characteristics.

However, the book can also be a valid in-depth tool for the more experienced, especially as regards the psychological aspects related to money, investments and success.

Reading this book alone won't make you a pro. It is however the solid basis on which to base your future in-depth studies.

Keep this in mind as you read through this book and begin investing your money.

We wish you luck!

What Is Financial Literacy?

Financial literacy is something that everyone has deep inside of them; however, not many people know how to use it to their full potential.

Some people have more awareness of financial literacy and are naturally better at using their money to create more money.

Being financially intelligent does not mean that you have to work yourself to the bone; it simply means that you need to have a certain set of skills to help you work smartly.

These skills are generally in the form of self-discipline, mindset, and good habits.

The more financial literacy you have, the easier it will be for you to understand how to work with your money.

In most cases, successful self-made people are always those with high financial literacy.

So let's first define financial literacy.

The term financial literacy describes a person's competence at understanding the various financial situations' ins and outs; this can vary from your company's finances or personal finances.

In this book, you will greatly improve your financial literacy, and you will begin to see the effects of this in your life!

What Is Financial Independence?

Financial independence is achieved when a person no longer has to work hard to make money actively to pay their bills and survive.

Further, if any unexpected incident happens like a flooded basement or an illness, you have enough saved to cover the associated costs.

Financial independence simply means that a person doesn't have to worry about paying rent or their electric bill anymore, and they have some money saved for a rainy day on top of that.

Financial freedom means that you no longer have to work hard to make money actively to pay your bills and survive, similar to financial independence.

When a person is financially free, it usually means that they no longer have to stress or worry about money in any way.

Becoming financially free may sound simple, but this differs significantly in different people.

Some people may define themselves as financially free if they have enough income coming into support for their traveling, partying, and fancy vacations.

To other people, their specific goals for financial freedom may be different.

The bottom line is that you have more than enough money to support your lifestyle, and in the event of anything unexpected, you do not have to worry.

What Is Early Retirement?

Early retirement is something that many people strive for but that few can achieve.

This book will teach you how to achieve it and set you up for success in the best way possible. First, what is defined as early retirement?

Early retirement is most often defined as retirement before the age of 65- or when the government would begin to legally support or assist you as a retiree.

Of course, this number depends on where you live in the world, but this is the definition in North America.

What Will You Learn in This Book?

Throughout this book, I will teach you about all the skills you will require to become a successful entrepreneur. In the first half of the book,

I will be covering various financial strategies that you may find helpful for your business.

In the second half of the book, I will teach you how to develop the right mindset, habits, and productivity required to achieve success.

These two parts of the book work hand in hand to ensure you are a well-rounded entrepreneur who has both the mindset and the financial skills to build a successful business.

It's completely okay if you are just starting in your career and you lack the financial background.

As I mentioned, your mindset and habits are also an important part of this equation, so stay persistent and driven, and you will be unstoppable.

Chapter 1: Passive Income

We will begin the book by learning about something called *passive income*.

After reading this chapter, you should have a firm grasp of this concept and how it will help you retire early and achieve financial independence for life!

Without further ado, let's begin.

What Is Passive Income?

To understand passive income, we must first understand active income.

Active income means that the income you receive is for a series of services that you have performed.

Examples of active income include; salaries, wages, commissions, tips, and business endeavors.

Examples of this would be someone working as a teller at the bank. They get paid in salary, and they are getting paid in exchange for the services they perform for one specific company.

Another example would be a waiter working at a restaurant; the wages they earn per hour are their active income, so are the tips they make.

They actively perform services for one specific establishment and are an employee of the business.

Passive income is a type of income that derives from a business or enterprise where the person is not actively involved.

Passive income may include income from a rental property, a company they share in or renting out their car on share websites.

In the simplest terms, active income means that you are physically doing something to obtain income, whereas passive income means you are 100% hands-off or close to it.

From this definition of passive income, I'm sure you can see how beneficial this can be for your life and your financial future, but in the next section, I will share with you how anyone can achieve this.

What Is a Side Hustle?

One of the best ways to create a steady source of passive income for yourself is to develop a side hustle.

A side hustle is like a second job or a side job that provides you with an additional source of income, along with your day job.

Rather than being employed by someone else or another company on the side, the best type of side hustle is a business that you open yourself 'on the side' that will act as a passive income source for you.

This passive income source will allow you to work your regular hours while making much more money.

Your side hustle could be a passion project or simply an additional method that you use to help supplement your income without adding additional work hours to do so.

Side hustles are not the same as a part-time job. At a part-time job, your employer will be managing your time and how much pay you receive.

On the other hand, side hustles give you the freedom to decide how much you want to earn and how many hours you want to work.

With financial security becoming a considerable problem for nearly 50% of America, side hustles have become a popular option for people looking to get out of debt or are just interested in starting their own business.

However, don't get confused with a side hustle being a full-blown standalone business – most people who start their side hustle still have to work a traditional full-time job.

The reason for this is that side hustles may not generate any income until you get the proper traction and marketing.

Having a full-time job enables you to have the ability to pay your bills while also spending some of your free time building your side-hustle, so eventually, it does start creating a separate stream of income.

So how does a side hustle work? You will work to build your side hustle during the hours outside of your day job.

In the beginning, you will need to spend some time building your side hustle, so your working hours for your side hustle will likely take place during weekends, evenings, or holidays.

After your side hustle business becomes well-established, however, you can begin to scale back your hours and transition to gaining solely passive income from this side hustle.

The Importance of Passive Income for Retiring Early and Finding Financial Independence

Did you know that the majority of families in America have about fifteen-thousand dollars or more in debt, specifically from credit cards?

Thanks to the spending culture that the Western world has fostered, people tend to spend money that they don't have through the use of credit cards and loans.

Side hustles are a great way to make extra money to pay off existing debt and to begin building a savings account that you can use to generate more money in the future.

In our modern world, other businesses have created numerous platforms that help match people with specific work skills that require it.

Thanks to these platforms, about 10% of people have their side hustles in our present day.

In the next section, we will be talking about all the different types of passive income sources out there, and you will have a better idea of which one suits you best.

Examples of Passive Income Streams and Their Earning Potential

In this chapter, we will look at ways to create a side gig for yourself that will ultimately become your passive income source.

E-Commerce?

Let's start by learning a little about online stores, how they can be side gigs and some of their benefits. Online stores are similar to popular e-platforms like Amazon and eBay.

However, the ones that can be utilized as side-gigs are typically on a smaller scale where sellers can post items they've made or second-hand items up for sale.

There are numerous amounts of online store platforms that are extremely user-friendly and can help you make money by selling your old items or hand-made items.

The first benefit that comes with using online stores as your side gig is time. You don't have to invest a lot of time into it; all you need to do to get started on most of these platforms are the following:

1. **SIMPLY MAKE AN ACCOUNT**
2. **BEGIN WITH A FEW ITEMS THAT YOU'D LIKE TO SELL**
3. **MAKE A POST**
4. **REPLY TO THE INTERESTED PEOPLE**

Yes, it's that simple.

However, you have to keep in mind that some items receive more attention from customers than others.

For instance, Apple products or any type of decently new electronics tend to get a lot of online attention. These products do well on second-hand online platforms like Letgo, Craigslist, and eBay.

If you are artistically skilled and can make homemade crafts like jewelry, pottery (mugs, vases, bowls), knits, etc., you can utilize more specialized websites like Etsy.

Let's dive into the different ways that you can begin to make money using online stores.

Dropshipping is a fairly new business model that people can use to run their online stores.

Dropshipping is simple; essentially, you have your online store with items of your choice to sell.

You also have a relationship with a wholesaler that can sell your products at wholesale prices.

You could sell items including watches, mugs, clothing, electronics, anything you can dream of really.

Once a customer purchases an item from your store, you will then purchase your item from the wholesaler and have the wholesaler mail that item to your customer directly.

You don't have to hold any inventory in your home with dropshipping or make many items from scratch.

For instance, if you have a Shopify store selling watches and your wholesaler sells you watches for $15 and sells them to customers for $40, you are making $25 of profit for every watch.

You also benefit from not having to pre-buy inventory, so you minimize the risk of producing a loss.

What I mean by this is the traditional way to run an online store is to have an inventory for things, right?

Let's stick with the same example; let's say you wanted to run an online watch business, and you bought ten watches for this season to sell at $15 each.

However, by the end of the season, you only sold five watches at $40 each.

Selling this way means that you spent $150 on your inventory and only made $200; that's a $50 profit, with five watches that are now out of season.

Dropshipping allows you to minimize your risk by purchasing items and selling them as the orders come in, therefore, maximizing your profit.

In the same example of watches, if you only had five orders for that season and bought five watches as those orders came in, you have made a $125 profit compared to the measly $50 profit.

Platforms that allow you to utilize the dropshipping method are Shopify, Amazon, and Alibaba.com.

Online Courses

This type of side gig is a new addition to the world of side gigs and has increased in popularity over the last 1 – 2 years.

This side gig makes you money by providing courses to people who require them to qualify for jobs and further education.

Platforms like udemy.com, teachable.com, and foundr.com offer courses that are made by other people at a discounted rate to either help people catch up on their credits or give them a certification that will allow them to qualify for their line of work.

Depending on what education you have or use this knowledge to create specific courses that people will pay to take.

Another option you have that is similar to the above is to create courses that you can use as a passive income source, but doing so without using a platform.

That way, you won't have to pay fees to the platform to host your courses.

The challenge here will be finding clients to purchase your courses, but if you are confident that you can develop leads and find business, this could be a great option for you.

ou can do this by hosting courses on your website and including a payment option.

Overall, course creation side gigs are beneficial to those who have a passion for teaching and are semi-skilled in course creation.

This type of work gives the freelancer a great opportunity to make large sums of money, but there is a high-risk factor.

If you put in 5 hours building your course for sale and you don't make any sales at all, then you just lost out on the time you put in when you could have used that time for other side gigs with a guaranteed return.

As I mentioned throughout this chapter, don't use online course creations as your main income source.

Combine it with other sources and analyze how well your sales are doing in the background before jumping all-in.

Keep in mind that flexibility is great in course creation gigs.

Due to its nature, you can do this type of work anytime you want as long as you have a computer that will allow you to do so.

There are no tight deadlines, and you can post courses for sale whenever you want.

This option could be a very good option for a fairly busy creative who wants a passive income source to pay their bills and make extra income.

Once you post your course online, you are hands-off, and you can wait for people to purchase it.

Book Sales

One great way to benefit from content writing in a passive form is by writing pieces and uploading them to various locations, which will earn you money.

For example, if you write an e-book, you can sell it on amazon or other e-book hosting locations.

This way, your book will make money each time someone buys it, and this provides you with passive income.

Online Content Creation

Online side gigs often involve creating content for people to enjoy.

This content can include videos, pictures, or anything you can show on the internet to curious viewers and scrollers.

There is a large market for content creation today since the internet and social media have such a massive presence in our society.

If you can take advantage of this, you can provide yourself with an income source by merely posting content on the internet.

Once you develop a following for yourself, you can begin to make money by giving this following with pictures and videos of yourself.

You will get paid through advertising and views, which is an excellent way to make passive income.

A Note on Side Gigs and Earning Potential

I want to note that to find success in your side gigs, don't silo yourself into just one type.

You should always have at least two side gigs ongoing so that if one gig is slow in business, you could tap into your other gig more.

Having only one side gig puts you at the risk of not being able to pay your bills if it's slow in business for one month.

In the scenario that you have started a side gig that you don't enjoy or doesn't meet the earning potential you imagined, then I encourage you to try a few others.

Finding the perfect side gig that you enjoy, pays well, and allows you to balance your time as a musician takes trial and error.

Don't give up just because the first side gig you tried didn't meet your expectations, try something else, and keep at it until you find one that works for you.

The side gigs in this book will also vary in terms of start-up costs. Some may require you to invest in equipment or tools, while others only require your body!

Again, depending on your resources, you may qualify for more or fewer of these options.

Keep in mind that choosing your line of business as an entrepreneur is important as well.

For instance, if your dream is to start a brewery, you must know about beer and beverage production.

If not, it is still possible to achieve this goal, but you need to invest more time into learning these skills from scratch.

Choosing the business you want to create has to be strategically based on your existing skills and background. It is okay to choose something that you have no experience in, but you must be prepared to commit the time and energy into a steeper learning curve.

For instance, if you have experience in landscaping, then starting your own landscaping business or renovations business may be the most strategic move for you.

On the other hand, choosing to start your restaurant may not be the best move for you, considering you don't have any existing skills.

How to Choose a Source of Passive Income

The first step in choosing a passive income source is to examine the resources you have access to.

It is essential to talk about your current resources and examine whether you have enough of these resources to support your perfect side hustle.

For instance, if you are interested in starting a business, it will not provide you with passive income at first until you get it established, so you must make sure you have a secure day job that can support you while you get your side hustle going.

1

WHAT ARE YOUR FINANCIAL RESOURCES?

Now, if you have many resources to work with, there are much easier ways to generate passive income without starting a business first.

We will spend most of this book discussing the investment options you have once you have enough financial resources to invest.

Still, this chapter will set you up to begin making extra money that you can later use to invest. More on this later.

2

WHAT PHYSICAL RESOURCES DO YOU HAVE?

Side gigs will vary in terms of their individual start-up costs. Some may require you to invest in equipment or tools, while others only require your body!

Depending on your resources, you may qualify for more or fewer of these options.

For example, are you able-bodied?

Do you have some physical resources available already, like a video camera, a car, a second property, a computer, or equipment to run a business of your choice?

These resources will influence your choices for starting a side hustle.

Moreover, depending on your resources, it will open up doors for your side gig options.

For instance, if you have a car, you will qualify to do numerous side gigs requiring a vehicle.

If you have a spare house or property, this opens up multiple options for you as well.

However, if you are someone with very limited resources, you may have to stick to the side gigs that do not require much equipment. This point is important to keep in mind so that you can make the most of the resources you have and set yourself up for success.

3

WHAT SKILLS CAN YOU USE TO MAKE MONEY?

The next step in choosing a side hustle or a passive income source is to examine your skills.

If you have the skill to start a specific or niche side business, this will provide you with a higher earning potential than a side hustle that does not require any specific skills.

It is beneficial to consider that option first when choosing a side hustle, as it is more suitable for your knowledge, skills, and income.

For instance, many different sides hustle out there, ranging from blog platforms to teaching personal training.

These side hustles require specific skills and have the potential to earn you an extra income of $500 - $4000 per month.

Some businesses have created numerous platforms aimed at matching people with specific side hustles based on work skills in our modern world.

Thanks to these platforms, you can easily find clients and consumers.

Passive Income Will Set You up for Investing Later on

As I mentioned in the previous section regarding resources, having financial resources will be necessary to make investments that will later pay off in big ways.

These investments include stocks, real estate, and so on. Suppose you are not at the point where you can invest your money just yet, start by developing a side hustle that will provide you with extra income.

Then, when you are ready, you can begin taking the advice I will provide you with over the next several chapters about how to grow that money for early retirement.

Have you ever heard the saying, "your first million is the hardest?" this is because money begins to make itself when you have enough of it.

For this type of person, you will be more interested in the financial realm of passive income, such as Stocks, Bonds, Commodities, and so on.

We will discuss this in chapter four, but for now, keep in mind that you can essentially start making passive income immediately if you have a lump sum of money.

For instance, if you have a small fortune saved up, think like $20,000.

You can easily put that $20,000 into high-interest savings account at your local bank and generate 2-3% interest on it monthly.

Doing this means that you are making $4,800 - $7,200 yearly by doing nothing at all. Although breaking it down into a monthly income, it's not much.

That being said, simply just putting your money in a high-interest savings account can make you as much as any other new side hustle can.

This method is the easiest way to make a passive income, but you could make even more money by doing other things that are more elaborate.

We will look at several examples, such as buying a rental property or renting your car.

How Passive Income Will Allow You to Retire Early

If you want to make enough money to retire early, the income you make from your day job will not be enough on its own.

However, with the help of passive income, you can create a situation for yourself where you have two different sources of income working together to speed up the process of achieving your goal.

If you have goals that require a lot of money, then creating multiple sources of passive income on top of your active income may be the ideal route.

However, if your goals do not require large sums of money, then maybe you can even comfortably live off of one source of passive income in addition to your day job.

I have a feeling that if you are reading this book, you are likely someone that is ambitious and is looking to create more streams of income to achieve big dreams involving financial freedom, early retirement, and a good life free of financial stress.

So, throughout this book, we will talk about how to get you there!

Chapter 2: Financial Literacy

This chapter will teach you about some aspects of financial intelligence (or financial literacy) that will help you increase your financial literacy and help you move onto more complex topics in the chapters that follow.

The Benefits Of Financial Intelligence

1. **FINANCIAL INTELLIGENCE CAN HELP YOU INCREASE YOUR WEALTH**

Everybody wants to increase their wealth; that is a common fact.

Those with high financial intelligence are simply more natural at doing it.

Regardless of whether you are an entrepreneur or not, managing your money is important.

People make a lot of money out of their existing money simply because they can control their cash flow at all times.

You don't have to own a business to be financially intelligent; keeping track of your personal expenses and managing that is enough to grow your financial intelligence.

2. FINANCIAL INTELLIGENCE CHANGES THE WAY YOU RELATE TO MONEY

As we mentioned earlier, your mindset is crucial to your entrepreneurial success.

However, your mindset is also very important and has a large effect on your financial intelligence and success.

Successful money people control their money, and they don't let their money control them.

They decide where the money goes and doesn't allow money to determine where they go.

Financially intelligent people are not afraid of money; they usually have complete control over all their finances.

3. FINANCIALLY INTELLIGENT PEOPLE HAVE KNOWLEDGE ABOUT MONEY

There is a big difference between what you know about money and what your beliefs are about money.

Most people only understand the purchasing power that money brings, and that's about it.

However, financially intelligent people know more than just that. They understand what their assets are and what their liabilities are.

They understand the difference between a credit and a debit card, and usually, it's the lack of knowledge that causes people to make financial mistakes leading them to be in huge debt.

4. FINANCIALLY INTELLIGENT PEOPLE KNOW WHAT TO DO WITH THEIR MONEY

Most people think that they aren't making enough money; although this is true in some cases, many people are not utilizing their money correctly.

When you aren't utilizing your money correctly, people often believe that they are not making enough.

The caveat to this is that the more money a person makes, the more inclined to spend they will be.

Financially intelligent people are not constantly chasing after more people; they typically find success by controlling their earnings.

Typically, a financially intelligent person would aim to save at least 10% of their income, and they never touch it.

That 10% is saved for investment purposes or kept as emergency money.

5. FINANCIALLY INTELLIGENT PEOPLE HAVE BOTH SHORT AND LONG TERM GOALS

When it comes to money goals, financially intelligent people usually have a set of short term and long term goals.

The ability to differentiate between these two types of goals will keep you balanced and focused.

People typically forget about their larger goals when faced with simpler and more easily-achievable shorter-term goals.

To build future wealth, you MUST remain focused on your longer-term goals just as you work on your closer or smaller goals.

Typically, short-term goals would be saving up for a 2-week vacation, while long-term goals would be saving up for a mortgage or business investment.

If you spend the first $2,000 you save on a vacation, none of that money will ever touch your long-term goals. Financially intelligent people make sure to always be achieving both without losing sight of either.

Financial Terms and Information for Entrepreneurs or People With Side Hustles

I will be teaching you about important financial terminology.

These are numbers that you need to know to run a successful business. I will also teach you how to properly understand them and analyze the meaning of these numbers.

You will be learning about ROI, margins, break-evens, and fixed/variable costs.

Don't worry; I will also teach you how to calculate each of these numbers.

Let's get started.

- **RETURN ON INVESTMENT (R.O.I.)**

Whether you are an investor or business owner, return on investment is an important analytical tool that you will need to use.

The definition of ROI is the relationship between a loss and a profit/loss during the fiscal year of a business.

This term is described as an investment.

Financial Metric	Case Alpha	Case Beta
Net Cash Flow	$140	$120
Return on Investment **ROI**	29.5%	51.1%
Future Performance	Improving	Neutral
Payback Period	3.14 Yr	1.50 Yr
Net Present Value **NPV**	$70.51	$76.18
Internal Rate of Return **IRR**	29.9%	44.9%

This number is always written or described as a percentage increase or decrease related to the investment value during that fiscal year.

Here is a simple example: imagine that you invest $200 in stocks, and the value of those stocks increases to $220 by the end of that fiscal year.

In this example, your ROI would be 10%.

In one more complicated example, if you invested $1000 in coffee bean stock for your coffee business and at the end of the year you generated $2200 from selling coffee made by the beans (assuming no other costs or taxes are involved), your ROI is 220%.

Here is the formula for ROI:

(Profit / Investment) x 100% =

Return On Investment

We will now use this equation in a different example.

Imagine that you are in the business of flipping houses.

You purchased a cheap house at $75,000, and then you paid $35,000 for materials for upgrades to the house.

When the house's sales, commission, and expenses are all considered, you made

$160,000 on this house. What would be your ROI?

First, you have to calculate your net profit, your total revenue subtracted from your total costs.

In this case, that would be $160,000 − ($75,000 + $35,000), this gives you $50,000. Remember, your costs are the purchase of the house ($75K) and the money you spend on materials ($35K).

Since Return On Investment = Profit/Investment x 100

ROI = (50,000/110,000) x 100

ROI = 45 x 100

ROI = 45%

This equation may make house flipping sound easy but remember it is also possible to lose your money when investing it like this. Imagine your investment is, in fact, a loss.

This equation will give you a number that is below zero. After everything, you could only sell the house for $90,000 as there are no other buyers.

Take a look at the new ROI:

Revenue − Total Cost = Net Profit

$90,000 - $110,000 = -$20,000

ROI = Profit/Investment x 100

ROI = (-20,000/110,000) x 100

ROI = -0.182 x 100

ROI = -18.2%

Essentially, you want your business to be yielding a positive number from your ROI; the higher, the better.

If you yield a negative number, you may have to start rethinking your business plan or lower the business cost.

- **MARGINS**

In the world of finance, there are various types of margins.

The one that is most popularly used is the Profit Margin. There are also other kinds that we will look at below.

Usually, you can come up with a number to represent the profit of a business in 3 categories.

These will all be displayed on their income statement.

Firstly, would be their gross profit.

Next, and the best in terms of being comprehensive, is the business's net profit.

Additionally, you will find their operating profit.

- **GROSS PROFIT MARGIN**

We are going to begin by looking at the gross profit margin. The GPM describes the profit of a business after accounting for;

The (COGS) or the cost of goods sold.

COGS includes the expenses that are DIRECTLY related to production and manufacturing, such as labor wages and raw materials.

For instance, if you are a coffee bean seller, your COGS will be the cost of coffee beans purchased.

Other figures are excluded in this figure, such as taxes, debt, overhead costs, operating costs, and large expenditures like equipment purchase.

- **OPERATING PROFIT MARGIN**

  The operating profit margin is slightly more complex as it considers all other expenses such as; sales expenses, administrative expenses, operating expenses, and overhead expenses.

  These are all expenses that are necessary to keep the business running on a day-to-day business.

  This figure, however, still excludes non-operational expenses like debts and taxes.

  However, it DOES include the depreciation and amortization of assets.

- **NET PROFIT MARGIN**

  So the net profit margin, otherwise known as the well-known "bottom line."

This number is the revenue (in dollars) that is remaining once every expense and type of income is calculated for.

This amount will include the operational expenses we just talked about, COGS, and other expenses such as taxes, debts, and other payments.

This number reflects a business's ability to generate profit from their income.

- **COSTS**

Now, let's learn about fixed and variable costs.

There are 2 primary costs that a business has.

These costs include variable costs and the fixed costs.

The variable cost differs based on the amount a business is producing, while the fixed costs remain the same regardless of how much output the business is producing. Let's take a look at variable cost first.

- **VARIABLE COST**

This term is used to describe the number of services or the amount of goods that a business is producing.

This cost will decrease or increase based on the production volume.

When business production increases, the variable cost will rise. If the business product decreases, then the variable cost will decline.

Variable costs will differ widely between various industries.

This variation means that it is not useful for you to compare a coffee shop's variable costs to a car manufacturer because their product output is entirely different.

It is easier to look at two businesses within one industry when making comparisons, such as two coffee shops.

The number for a business's variable cost is arrived at by multiplying the output by the cost per unit of output.

For instance, let's say company A produces ceramic plates for $2 per plate.

If this business creates 500 units, the variable cost is $1000.

On the other hand, if the business has no orders and therefore does not produce any plates, then the variable cost would be $0 if the company gets a large order of 10,000 plates, the cost increases and becomes $20,000.

This number does not take into account other costs, such as raw materials or labor.

- **FIXED COST**

The other type of cost that any business or company will have is the Fixed Cost.

Different from the variable cost, the fixed cost doesn't change based on the number of units produced. It will remain consistent when the business produces zero goods.

This concept means that this cost cannot be avoided.

Let's use the same example for company A.

Imagine that Company A's fixed cost is $10,000 per month, which includes their plate producing machine rental.

If the company has no orders for that month and doesn't produce any plates, they still have to pay $10,000 for the machine rental.

However, let's imagine that they get a massive order of one million plates, the rental of that machine remains the same; $10,000.

However, the variable cost will be $2M in this example.

The higher the fixed cost is for a company, the more revenue they will require to break even.

This number means that the company will need to sell more products and work harder because these costs usually are unable to be lowered.

The most common fixed costs examples are; building leases/rent payments, certain salaries, interest payments, insurance, and utilities.

Variable costs tend to remain consistent based on the number of goods the company produces, but the effects of fixed costs on the business's bottom line will differ according to how many goods are made. If they produce a lot, fixed cost decreases.

The cost of a larger number of goods is spread out across the entirety of the fixed cost.

Due to this, a business could achieve "economies of scale."

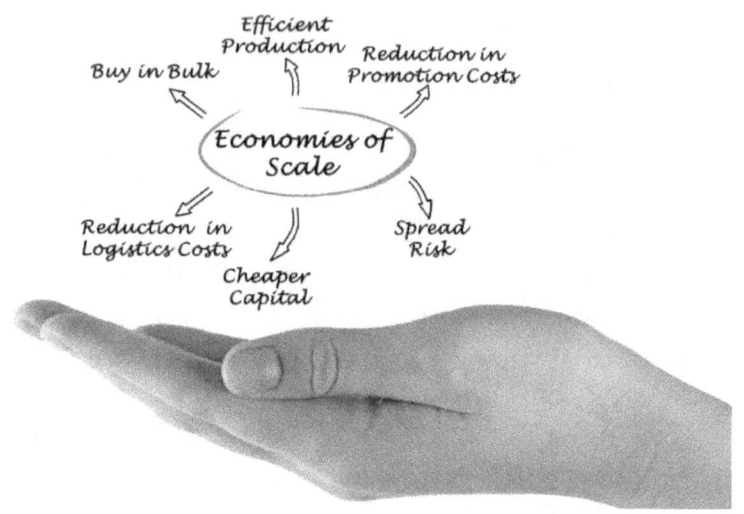

As an example; Say company A has a $10,000 monthly lease for the factory it uses.

Say this company makes 1000 plates each month.

This business will spread its fixed cost (the lease), making it $10 per plate. ($10,000/1000 plates)

However, if company A produces 10,000 plates per month, then its lease's fixed cost goes down to $1 per plate.

Understanding Basic Financial Statements

In this subchapter, I will be teaching you how to read and analyze your basic financial statements.

These statements are usually; income statements, balance sheets, and cash flows.

If you are someone who has gone to business school or taking finance/accounting at a college or university level, you probably already know this information.

If not, you will want to pay extra attention.

This section will apply to you even more once you start your own business or begin investing your money.

Let's start by learning income statements first.

Income Statements

An income statement is a bare minimum that you would need to know for you to manage your business's finances. An income statement's purpose is simple; it tells you whether you are profiting or losing money. Here is an example of a very simple income statement of a child's allowance:

Revenue or Gross Income: $5.00

Expenses: $2.00 (Candy)

Net Income: $3.00

See how simple this is?

The first line includes money coming into your possession, while the second line is the money going out of your possession.

The bottom line is the difference between the two.

Since the number is positive, it means you are making money. If the net income is negative, it means you are losing money.

Income statements can be as simple as such, but it does get more complicated the larger your company gets.

INCOME STATEMENT EXAMPLE

TOTAL REVENUE	$150,000
COST OF GOODS SOLD	(25,000)
GROSS PROFIT	125,000

OPERATING EXPENSES	
PAYROLL	15,000
UTILITIES	10,000
RENT	15,000
DEPRECIATION	10,000
TOTAL OPERATING EXPENSES	(50,000)
INTEREST	(15,000)
TAXES	(15,000)
NET PROFIT	45,000

As companies grow larger and larger, they include a few more variations of the same structure.

For instance, they may have additional lines such as; "cost of revenue" or "gross profit."

They may also have additional lines differentiating their income, such as; "operating income" or "income before taxes."

Entrepreneurs need to ensure that their income statements are accurate because they need to see whether their business is succeeding or not.

An inaccurate income statement can cause you to think that your business is making more than it is (bad scenario) or making less than you think it is (better scenario).

Balance Sheets

The balance sheet is simple to understand. Its purpose simply is to give you information regarding how healthy your business is currently.

There are three main numbers you should care about in a balance sheet:

1. **ASSETS**

2. **LIABILITIES**

3. **SHAREHOLDER'S EQUITY.**

Equity is simply the difference between assets and liabilities.

If you have more liabilities than assets, it means that your company is at a deficit.

If you have more assets than liabilities, then your company is at a surplus. Let's take a look at assets first.

Companies typically have current assets and non-current assets.

Firstly, a company's current assets include the items of value that a company owns, which are going to be converted to cash during the next year.

A company's current assets could encompass their; accounts receivable, inventory, and cash.

The accounts receivable means their outstanding invoices that include money owed to the company.

Inventory is a term used in companies that are selling products such as electronics, clothing, furniture, etc.

Cash can include physical cash, checks, and bank accounts that are not restricted.

Secondly, you will need to take a look at your non-current assets.

These include assets that will not or cannot be converted to cash within the next year.

These can be either physical or non-physical assets.

Physical assets are physical things like a business's equipment, machines, or property.

Intangible assets are non-physical things such as patents, copyrights, and goodwill.

Non-current assets are usually calculated with depreciation factored in, which is the asset's cost over its lifespan.

Thirdly, we have our liabilities. Liabilities are a company's financial obligations that are owed to someone else.

There are two types of this as well; current liabilities and long-term liabilities.

Current liabilities are short-term liabilities that need to be paid within one year; this includes; payments towards long-term debts, payroll, and accounts payable.

Long-term liabilities are financial obligations that will be due in more than one year, including loans and debts.

Lastly, there is your shareholder's equity. Shareholders equity means the complete net worth of the company.

Included in this is any sum of money that the owner invested at the beginning. If you decide to invest your first year's net earnings into your business, you will report those numbers under shareholders' equity.

Your balance sheets will typically be separated by 2 sides.

A balance sheet is correct when both sides equal one another.

Each of the sides on a balance sheet is; your assets and financial obligations.

> The main formula of this sheet isAssets = Liabilities + Shareholders Equity

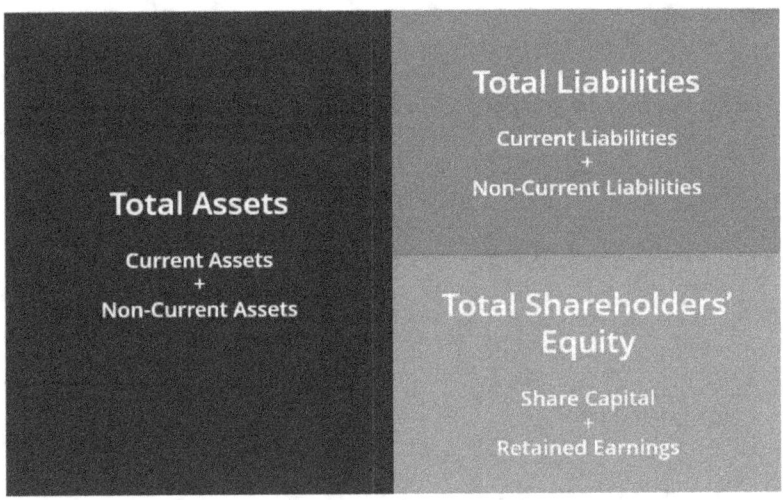

Here is a simple example of a balance sheet from a printing company.

ASSETS

- Current Assets:
  - Bank Account: $3470.00
  - Petty Cash: 50.00
  - *Total Current Assets: $3520.00*

- Fixed Assets:
  - Vehicle: $4500.00
  - Printer: 1800.00
  - *Total Fixed Assets: $6300.00*

- Inventory:
  - Stock: $1500.00

TOTAL ASSETS: $11,320.00

LIABILITIES

- Current Liabilities:
  - Accounts Payable: $1800.00
  - *Total Current Liabilities: $1800.00*

- Long Term Liabilities
  - Vehicle Loan: $4500.00
  - *Total Long Term Liabilities: $4500.00*

TOTAL LIABILITIES: $6300.00

EQUITY

- Initial Investment: $5000.00
- Drawings: -$130.00
- Current Earnings: $150.00
- Total Equity: $5020.00

Following the balance sheet equation:

Assets = Liabilities + Shareholders Equity,

our equation would look like this:

$$\text{Assets} =$$

$$\$6{,}300.00 +$$

$$\underline{\$5{,}020.00 =}$$

$$\$11{,}320.00$$

Therefore, our balance sheet is correct.

Cash Flows

The cash flow statement is crucial in all businesses as it shows us how the company is spending its money and where their money is coming from.

The cash flow statement will show you everything from all the cash it receives from its operations and all the cash that is leaving to pay for business costs and investments.

A cash flow statement **is comprised of 3 parts**: operations, investing, and financing.

Here is how a typical cash flow statement will look :

PART 1

CASH FLOW FROM OPERATIONS

The first part in the sheet shows us how much cash is coming from the income statement.

A few items under this heading include; payables, income taxes payable, and accounts receivables.

When your client makes a payment for their invoice, it will be completed as a receivable transaction, which means it will be recorded under operations.

Any changes in a company's current assets or liabilities are also recorded as cash flow from operations.

PART 2

CASH FLOW FROM INVESTING

The second type includes any cash flow as a result of purchases or sales of fixed assets or investments, such as equipment and property.

Examples of this would be purchases of land, furniture, vehicles, or buildings.

Usually, investing transactions will lead to cash outflows.

These would include; expenditures for equipment, property, plant, business acquisitions, or buying securities.

Cash inflows will result after sales of these assets.

PART 3

CASH FLOW FROM FINANCING

This section is where any debt and equity transactions will be reported.

All types of cash flows that include the repurchase/sale of bonds and stocks and dividends payment are considered cash flows for financing activities.

Cash that you receive from a loan or cash that you use to pay off a loan is also recorded in this section.

Here is a sample cash flow:

Michael's Food Delivery

August 2020

Cash Flows From Operating Activities

- Net Income: $98,285.71

- Receipts From Customers: $76,082.77

- Payments to employees and suppliers: -$32,846.13

- Total adjustments to reconcile net income to net cash provided by operations: $43,236.44

- *Total cash flows from operating activities: $141,522.35*

Cash Flows From Investing Activities

- Computer Equipment: -$1283.49

- Other cash items from investing activities: $2464.84

- *Total cash flows from investing activities: $1181.35*

Cash Flows Financing Activities

- Other cash items from financing activities: $5000.00

- *Total cash flows from financing activities: $5000.00*

<u>Net cash increase for the period: $147,703.70</u>

Cash Balances:

- Net cash increase for the period: $147703.70

- Cash at the beginning of the period: $52,819.91

- Cash at the end of the period: $200,523.61

How to Ensure That Your Side Hustle/Business Is Making You Money, Not Costing You Money

When starting a business, it is essential to track how much time you spend on it.

You must track this to determine your revenue and profits per hour.

Let's say you needed 10 hours of work to jumpstart your business (e.g., getting a website/social media built, advertising, business development), and you managed to get yourself your first two clients.

We are going to use the example of a coaching business to illustrate this concept.

Since coaching sessions are usually one hour in length and may happen 1 – 3 times a week, you need to divide your profit by how many total hours you've put into it.

For example, let's pretend that your two existing clients agree to three coaching sessions per week for an open-ended amount of time.

They may only need one month of coaching in total, or they may require several years, but they are playing that by ear.

Here are the numbers for this example:

10 hours (setting up the business)

2 Existing Clients (3 sessions per week)

$150 per session (1 hour)

In your first week of coaching your clients, the above points demonstrate that you have made ($150 x 3 sessions x 2 clients) $900.

This amount sounds like a lot, but if you divide it out by the amount of time you put in, your revenue per hour is only $56 per hour.

Of course, you have to keep in mind that the initial 10 hours that you've put into your business at the beginning is a one-time occurrence.

Still, you have to factor in the hours OUTSIDE of the sessions where you are scheduling, managing, and developing your business.

In other words, what I'm saying is that you must do these calculations before dedicating a generous amount of time to your business.

If there are other side hustles out there that don't require such a large amount of time and pay more than $56 per hour, you may want to consider those options too.

Be sure to look into all of these options before settling on a side hustle.

How to Save the Most Money Possible

Even if you manage to create a stream of passive income for yourself, you need to properly handle that new income source.

In this section, I will teach you how to handle your additional income to have enough money to invest, as we will discuss in the later chapters of this book.

On top of building better habits to help you spend money responsibly, there are other ways for you to save money.

This section will be walking you through a few money-saving tips that anyone can follow to increase their savings account.

Keep in mind; these tips are only helpful if you put them to use.

You may have bad habits surrounding what you buy and how you buy.

Use the self-discipline techniques you learned earlier in this book to put these money-saving tips into practice.

1. CUT DOWN ON GROCERY COSTS

If you don't already have a grocery budget, you need to start one now.

First, start calculating how much you usually spend on groceries every money.

If you're the average American family, you will likely spend around $650 every money on groceries.

That is a lot of money. You can cut down that spending by half.

It's very easy to just grab a bag of chips or a box of cookies that a) cost a lot of money and b) are not healthy and won't fill up your stomach. Save money on grocery costs by planning meals each week and assessing the products that your pantry already contains before heading to the grocery store.

Alternatively, grocery stores now offer online orders so you can pick your groceries online before going to pick them up.

This method will help get rid of temptations that you get when you get into the store.

2. CANCEL YOUR AUTOMATIC SUBSCRIPTIONS

You likely have multiple subscriptions such as Netflix, Spotify, or gym memberships.

Assess which ones you do NOT use regularly (regular means you're using it several times per week).

Cancel it, and if you feel as if you really can't go without it, you can re-subscribe.

3. BORROW ITEMS, DON'T BUY THEM

If you require an item that you know you'll only use occasionally, like a tree trimmer or camping tent, borrow it from someone you know rather than buying a brand new item.

If you must buy an item, look for the same model or same item on a second hand buy/sell site.

If you don't use this item on the regular, sell it back via those websites.

This way, you are almost always breaking even every time you buy something 'new.'

4. ASK FOR DISCOUNTS/BARTER

If you're going to a well-established business such as the movie theatre, you may not be able to barter the price of your movie ticket.

However, you should ALWAYS ask if they have any discounts, deals, or coupons available at the moment.

Sometimes, if you have a membership with a gym or your AAA, they may have hidden discounts.

If you are shopping at a local farmer's market, be sure to barter.

Usually, they always offer discounts for people who want to buy in bulk.

5. LOWER YOUR CELL PHONE BILL

Believe it or not, many people's cellphone bills exceed $100 per month.

Try to cut that down as much as you can.

Save money on areas that are not completely necessary, like cellphone data, phone insurance, or additional warranties.

If your current provider cannot offer you any discounts or simply refuse to, look into switching providers and watch how quickly your original provider changes their mind! Also, you can switch your monthly plan to pay as you go plans.

That way, you aren't spending unnecessary money if you don't use your cellphone as much.

AND MORE....

Financial Independence, Retire Early
Dan Graham & Matthew Buffet

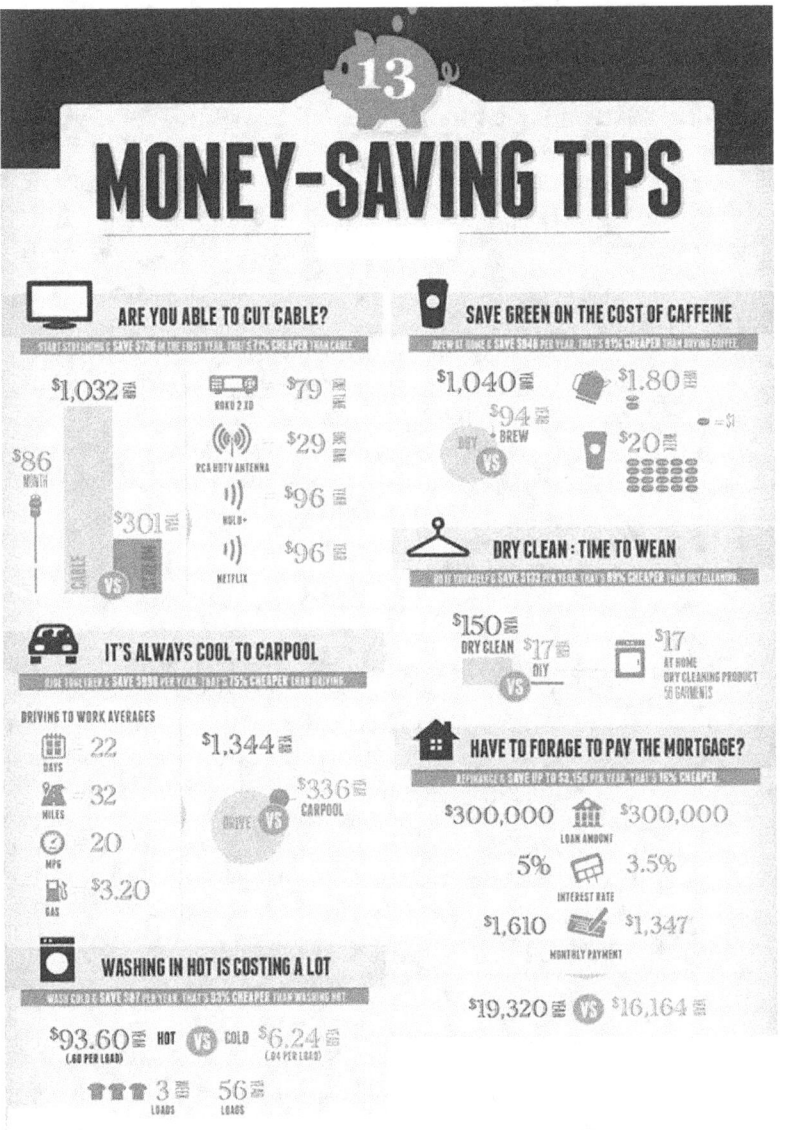

Financial Independence, Retire Early
Dan Graham & Matthew Buffet

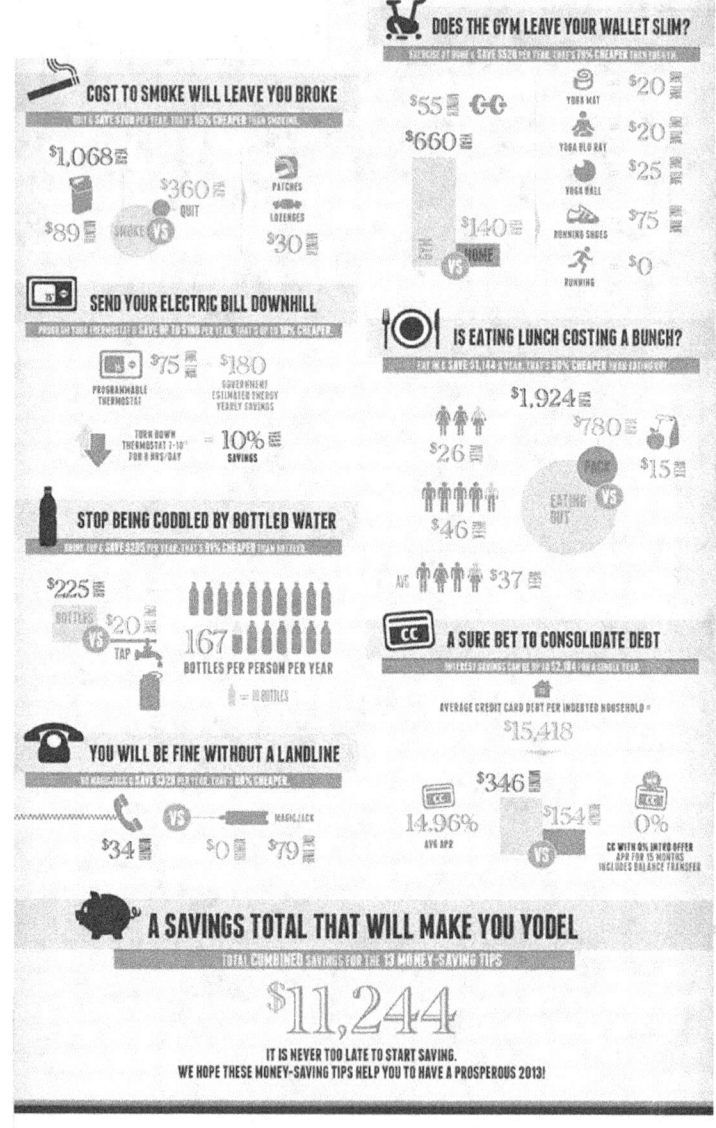

How to Use Goal Setting to Increase Chances of Success

If your main goal is to build sustainable wealth, then you must actively set and adjust all smaller goals along the way that will help you achieve your main goal.

Keeping your goals stagnant or refusing to break them down into smaller milestones will not only overwhelm you but can easily demotivate you.

Let's learn the difference between active goal setting and passive goal setting.

Passive goal setting means you are setting goals mentally, making them passive because of the lack of details involved.

It also means that a person hasn't properly defined their actual goal, which makes causes difficulty when it difficult to track progress and identify the tasks that need to be done to achieve that goal.

On the other hand, active goal setting is the complete opposite of passive goal-setting. Active goal setting means writing out your goals and ensuring an important meaning behind them.

Active goals are measurable and specific. To successfully create and make an active goal, you must build a plan towards achieving it.

This plan includes breaking down your goals into smaller tasks and steps that are clear and achievable.

Implementing active goal-setting into your daily life ingrains the discipline in us because you are forced to give it direction.

By breaking down your big goals into smaller daily goals, it helps people avoid distractions by only looking at what they need to get done in the present day.

This way, a person isn't left constantly thinking about one large intimidating goal but not knowing how to approach it.

Active goal setting works by getting you to take the first step in setting your long-term goals.

Do you currently know of any goals you want to accomplish?

If the answer is yes, you should begin actively participating in daily, weekly, and monthly active goal setting exercises.

You must play an active role in tracking your progress towards your goals and making changes in places where you feel like they aren't working.

Rather than just saying that your goal is to become a successful entrepreneur, you need to start planning exactly what steps you believe will take you there.

My advice for you will be to take out a pen and a piece of paper and start writing down what long-term goals you have.

Once you have some long-term goals written down, break them down into monthly, weekly, and daily goals.

Simply start by accomplishing your daily goals and when you reach the end of the month, assess to see if you have achieved your monthly goal through accomplishing your daily goals.

If you haven't, look back on your daily goals and see if there's anything you can change to achieve next month's goal.

How to Use This Income for Early Retirement

Now that you understand the basic financial terms you need to know going forward in your side hustle or building your own business, we will begin learning how to use the money you make in these avenues to retire early.

Over the next several chapters, we will look at different options for investing your money.

Before moving on, we will address the topic of procrastination.

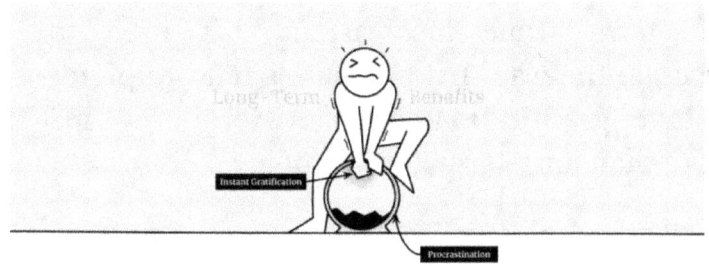

Procrastination can be very detrimental to you as you begin to make extra income through your side hustle, so I need to address it before discussing investments in more detail in the next chapter.

So, why is procrastination an entrepreneur's biggest enemy?

Let's learn more about the science behind this.

Through an abundance of psychology research, psychologists have discovered something that they call "time inconsistency."

This concept can explain the reasons that procrastination affects humans so largely by pulling us away from needed tasks no matter how much we want to do them.

The term "time inconsistency" is used to describe the way that our minds tend to prefer instant gratification or short-term rewards more than long-term gratification.

To illustrate this, we will look at an example.

Imagine that you have two alter egos.

The first is your current self, while the second is your future self.

When a person sets goals, such as getting fit by working out more or learning a new language, they make plans that they intend their future self to complete.

They plan ahead for what they hope their life to look like later on.

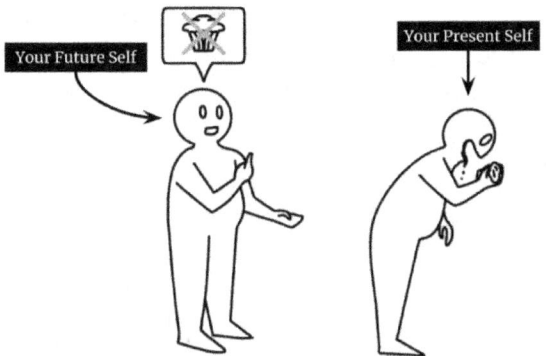

Evidence has shown that when a person thinks about their future self, their brain has no problem seeing the value of doing actions that will lead to long-term rewards.

The future self is the one that sees the merit in delaying gratification to achieve long-term benefits.

While the future self can only set goals, contrarily, the present self is the one that is responsible for taking action.

There will come a time where this individual will need to decide, but they aren't choosing the future self.

In the present moment, their brain is focused entirely on the present self.

Research shows that the present self prefers immediate rewards over long-term ones.

This thought process means that the present self and the future self don't get along or see eye to eye.

While your future self would prefer being healthy and having a six-pack, the present self wants some chili cheese fries.

Everyone knows that eating unhealthy will prevent health problems in the future when you're at an old age, but those things are so far away, so why worry about them now, right?

This idea s the thought process that many people have when faced with a choice of immediate gratification or achieving long-term goals.

Similarly, most adolescents understand that saving money for their retiree years during their 20s and 30s is extremely valuable, though the potential benefits of this are many years away.

It is much simpler for a person's current-self to understand the value of purchasing a new iPhone for themselves rather than putting away $1000 for their 75-year-old self!

This concept of "time inconsistency" may be the reason why people often go to sleep with motivation and inspiration to reach their goals and change their life.

Still, they find themselves completely falling back into bad habits when they wake up.

This effect happens because the human brain understands that long-term benefits are important when thinking about the future.

However it prefers instant gratification when thinking about and living out the present.

Procrastination plagues many of us in our daily lives, but since you are reading this book, you are likely looking to take action in your financial life. Please remember this as you make your way through the next several chapters, as the choices you make with your extra income will make or break your early retirement plan.

Chapter 3: Investment Funds

In this chapter, we will begin talking about how you can grow the money you have saved up!

This money can come from your savings account or from the income that you have made in your side hustle.

If you are going to create a source of passive income for yourself, you can use this income to invest.

Without further ado, I will begin by defining what an investment fund is.

The Benefits of Investing

Investing in a general sense is beneficial for a variety of reasons. Firstly, it allows you to grow the money you have earned much quicker than you can make it.

For example, imagine it would take you 10 years to make $20000 in savings by putting some money from every paycheck into a savings account.

Instead of making 20 thousand dollars in this way, you could invest five thousand dollars today and see it grow to 20 thousand dollars in much less time than 10 years.

In addition, by the time you have saved $20000, the impact of inflation would mean that your 20 thousand dollars would not be able to buy you nearly as much as it would today.

Below, you can see a chart illustrating the effects of inflation in the United States between the years 1913 and 2013.

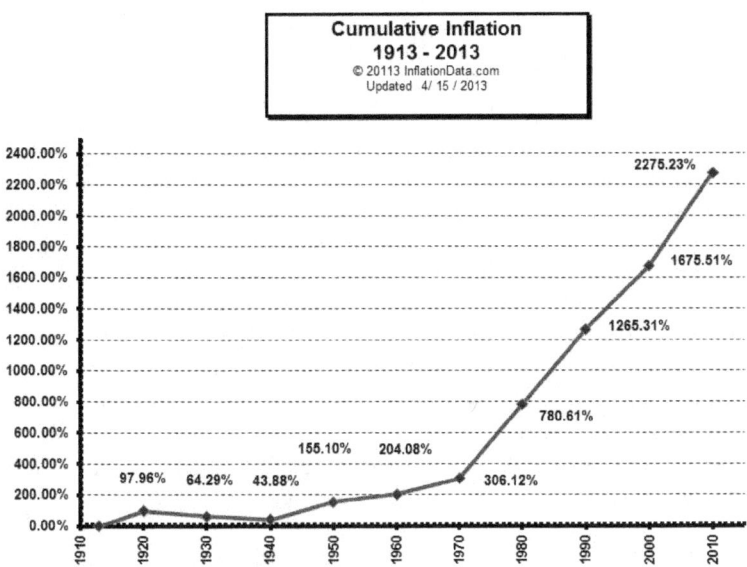

Another benefit of investing is the potential that it gives you to make large sums of money.

Even if you don't end up making it big and getting rich from your investments, it offers an opportunity to make additional, passive income that can help you and your family.

Working your day job will provide you with a regular salary, but investing will give you supplemental income on top of that.

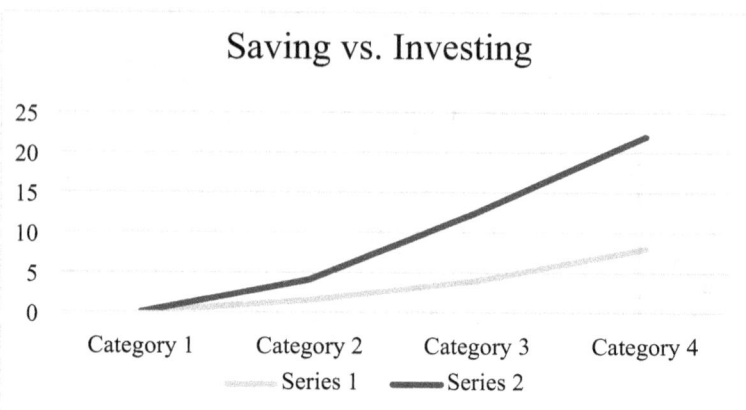

As you can see in the graph above, saving (series 1) grows much slower than investing (series 2).

What Is Capital?

Before defining what *investment funds* are, I must define the term *capital* for you.

Capital is a term used to describe assets. In this case, these assets are of the financial type.

Financial assets can include the following;

- **CASH**
- **FUNDS FROM FINANCING**
- **FUNDS IN DEPOSIT ACCOUNTS**
- **SECURITIES**
- **CASH EQUIVALENTS**

What Are Investment Funds?

Now that you understand what capital is, I will define investment funds for you. Investment funds are a type of capital that is held by many investors at the same time. These investors all maintain ownership of their shares of the capital.

The Benefits Of Investment Funds

Investment funds can provide you with numerous benefits, including the following;

- You can maintain control over your shares in the company or asset that you have invested in.

- The fees related to investing will be much lower when investing in investment funds than if you were to invest your money on your own.

- Your funds are managed by professionals, taking some of the work out of it for you, allowing you to rest easier than investing yourself.

- Gives you more opportunities for investing because the investment funds are shared amongst many people, allowing for more selection.

Examples Of Investment Funds And How To Use Them To Make Money

We will begin by looking at the options available to you regarding investment funds.

Once you understand your options, you can then make an informed decision about which works for you.

ETF (Exchange-Traded Fund)

An ETF (exchange-traded fund) is a type of investment fund that involves several securities like stocks. This group of securities follows a common theme.

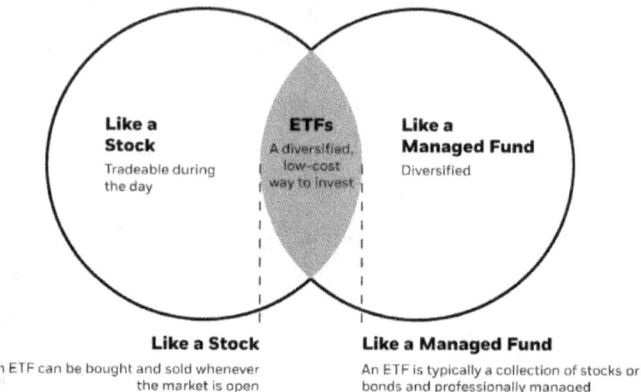

Low-Cost Funds

Lost cost funds are an investment option for those who do not want to part with large amounts of money upfront.

This kind of investment is a great option for risk-averse individuals, as these funds do not involve a person managing them, resulting in lower fees for investors.

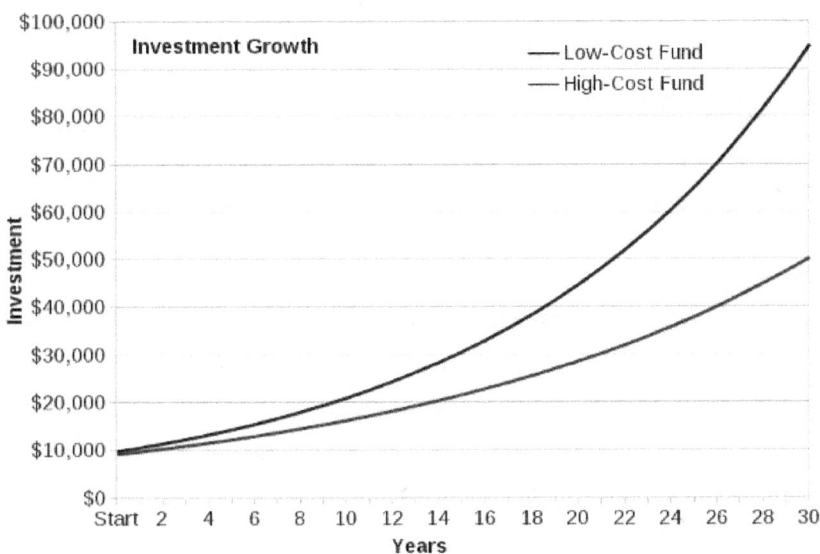

Stocks

Stocks are one of the most basic investment forms and likely the most common one you hear about.

In the most basic explanation, stocks are securities that represent an ownership share in a company.

Companies will issue stocks to raise money from the general public to grow and invest in their own business.

Stocks are then exchanged in the stock market.

The stock market, such as the New York Stock Exchange, is made up of exchanges.

Stocks are listed on a specific exchange and allow sellers and buyers to come together to sell/buy shares of certain stocks.

The exchange tracks the supply and demand, which usually directly relates to the price or each stock.

Stock prices fluctuate daily, and people who own stocks hope that stocks that they own will increase in value with time.

For instance, if you bought a stock for company A for $20 apiece, and that stock grows to be worth $50 apiece in three years, you have made $30 over three years ($10 per year).

However, stocks carry some of the highest risks than other investments, but they can also reap higher rewards.

Some people look at stocks as a type of 'gambling' as it is difficult to predict the increase/decrease of stocks.

Take a look at bitcoin; for example, what used to be a $7 stock grew to be worth $7000 per stock in the past few years.

Although this may sound promising, it can happen the other way around too.

You can buy a bitcoin stock for $7000 now and hope that it will grow to $14,000 or more.

However, it could drop down back to $7, causing you to lose significant amounts of money.

Financial Independence, Retire Early
Dan Graham & Matthew Buffet

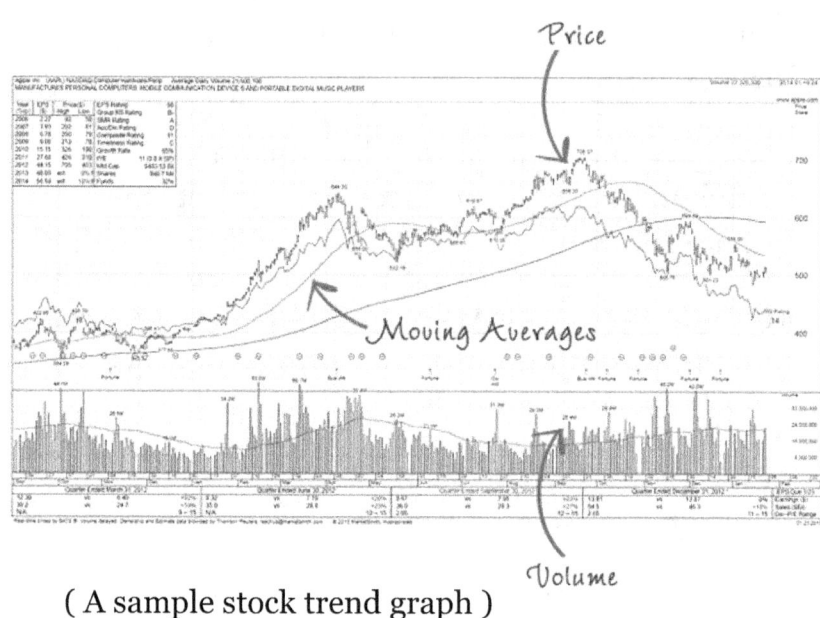

(A sample stock trend graph)

Bonds

Unlike a stock, a bond is a kind of loan that a company takes out, but instead of asking the bank for this money, they ask investors for money by asking them to purchase bonds.

As an exchange for the capital, the company will pay an annual interest rate on the bond, annually or semiannual, and then will return

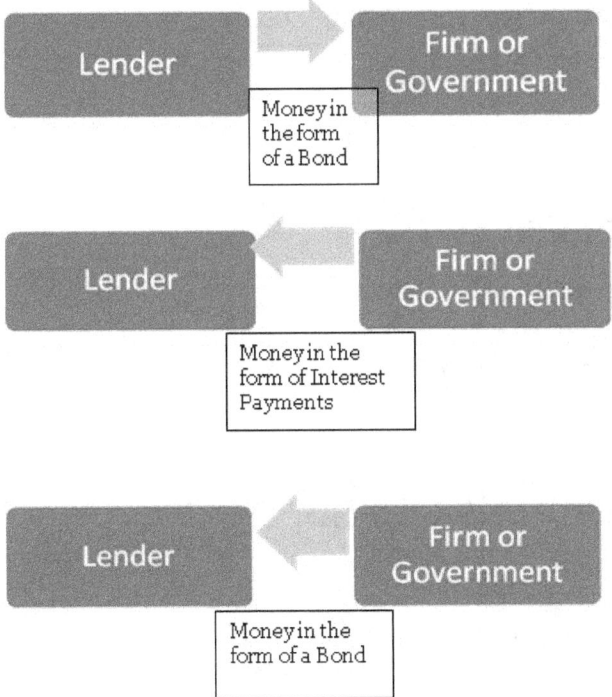

the principal loan when it reaches the date of maturity.

There are six features that you should look out for before purchasing a bond:

- **MATURITY:**

    Maturity refers to the date when the bond is paid, and when the initial chunk of money is returned to you.

    Maturity is often divided up into:

    short-term (1 – 3 years),

    medium-term (10+ years),

    and long-term (20+ years)

- **SECURED/UNSECURED:**

    This term describes the fact that a bond can either be secured or unsecured.

A secured bond promises the bondholders certain assets in the event that the company is unable to repay the money.

The term can also be described as "collateral."

If the firm cannot pay back its money, then the agreed-upon asset will go to the lender.

Unsecured bonds are the opposite.

Any collateral does not back them up.

These bonds will return only a small portion of the initial investment that you made if the company cannot pay back the money.

- **LIQUIDATION PREFERENCE:**

When a company declares bankruptcy, it will repay its investors following a specific order as they liquidate their assets.

Senior debt is what the company will repay first, and junior debt will be paid last.

Stockholders will then get the remaining money if there is any.

- **COUPON:**

    This term is used to describe the amount of interest that the company pays to bondholders on either an annual or semiannual basis.

    The Coupon can be referred to as the nominal yield or the 'coupon rate.'

    To calculate this, divide your annual payments by the face value of your bond.

- **TAX STATUS:**

    Most corporate bonds are included in taxable investments, but if the bonds are municipal or government bonds, they will be tax exempt.

Any income or gains will be taxed. However, tax-exempt bonds will have a lower interest rate than taxable bonds.

- **CALLABILITY:**

The company can pay off some bonds before its maturity. A company sometimes wishes to "call" the bonds if the interest rate allows for better borrowing rates.

Commodities

Commodities are part of any average American's life each day.

In its simplest form, a commodity includes a good that can be used in commerce to interchange with other goods in the same category.

For example, grains, beef, gold, natural gas, and oil are traditional commodities.

Commodities are an important way for investors to add variety into their portfolios past the traditional securities that are included.

Since commodity prices usually shift opposite the stocks, during periods of market volatility, investors most often rely on commodities.

Professional traders usually do commodity trading as it is more complicated and does require quite a bit of knowledge and education to pull off effectively.

For that reason, I won't go into detail about how commodities are traded and the functions.

401 (K)

A 401 (K) is a type of investment that involves a person's workplace. This type of investment involves a plan that your company will sponsor to match a portion of your contributions. This investment is a type of monetary plan for your retirement.

How important 401(k) benefits are to employees

- Very important, 62%
- Somewhat important, 26%
- Not too important, 8%
- Not at all important, 4%

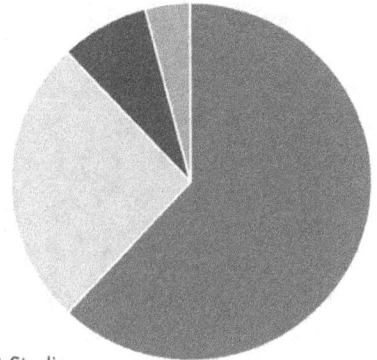

Source: Transamerica Center for Retirement Studies

TRF (Target-Risk Fund)

This kind of investment is a type of investment that involves a portfolio of a mix of stocks, bonds, and other types of investments.

This type provides the investor with a varied mix of investments in one package.

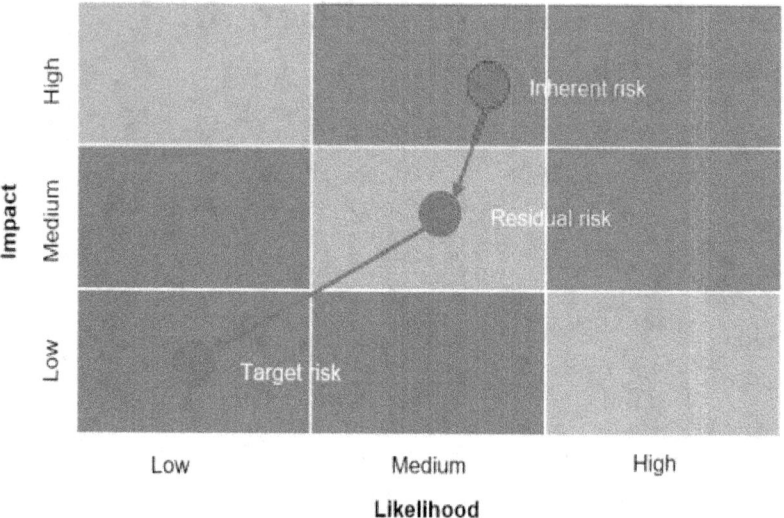

Mutual Funds

A mutual fund is a type of investment that involves a pool of money taken from multiple investors used to invest in things like bonds or stocks.

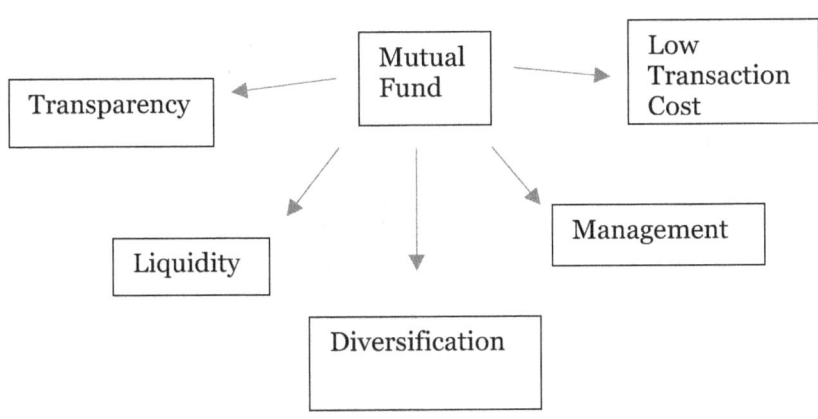

Hedge Funds

A hedge fund is an investment company that people provide their money with to invest in.

These hedge funds use the investors' money to purchase stocks or bonds while trying to beat the market or make experimental investments.

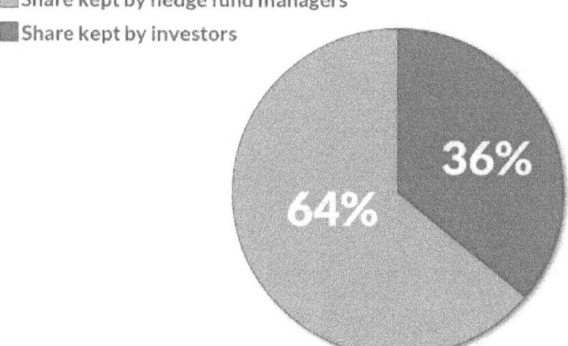

Who keeps the profits?
Relative shares of gross profits of hedge fund industry*

- Share kept by hedge fund managers
- Share kept by investors

36%
64%

*Based on study of nearly 6,000 hedge funds from 1995 through 2016

Source: Itzhak Ben-David, Justin Birru, Andrea Rossi

Where To Begin With Investing

Now that you understand the options available to you in terms of investments, we will look at how you can begin to benefit from them in your life.

When you are ready to begin investing, there are a few questions that you will need to ask yourself;

How Much Money do you Have to Invest?

Now, you may think that you need to have tens of thousands of dollars before you begin investing it.

This is not true, however. You only need a small amount of money to begin investing and growing it into a larger sum of money.

Keep in mind, the more you invest, the bigger it will grow, but if you don't have much to start with, that's okay too!

What are you Looking for in Terms of Return?

One of the first things that any investment broker will ask you when you begin to invest your money is how much risk you are willing to take.

This is an important question to ask yourself before you begin. If you want to take more risk, the rewards could be much higher, but the potential loss could also be great.

If you choose to remain more conservative in terms of risk, you may not gain as much as quickly, but you will not lose as much either.

Do you Want to Invest on your Own, or With a Broker?

There are a number of different ways to invest your money.

You can invest with a broker, on your own, or through your employer using a 401 (k) style investment.

Before you invest your money, ask yourself which of these three methods you prefer.

If you are just starting out, you may wish to use a broker so that you have someone to help you at each step of the process.

If you are confident in your financial investment knowledge and you feel comfortable, you can opt to invest alone.

When you decide that you want to invest with the help of a broker, there are a few different options available to you. You can go the route of a full-service broker, a discount broker, or a "robo-broker."

We will look at these 3 options below.

1. A full-service broker is the more traditional type of broker.

    This kind of broker will advise you and work with you on every investment you make.

    They will also talk to you about your goals related to retirement or your financial future.

    They will make a portfolio for you based on your preferred risk levels and your goals for the future.

    These brokers will charge a substantial fee, since they are very involved in the process, but you reap the benefits of this fee in terms of the help you get.

    Most of the time, these brokers will have minimum investments that they work with.

    For example, they may not work with investments under 25 thousand dollars, so keep this in mind.

2. A discount broker is an option that is becoming more popular these days.

   This kind of broker will give you advice and help you choose your investments wisely, but they are not as involved as a full-service broker would be.

   These brokers will provide you with the tools you need to invest, but at the end of the day, you make the decisions and the investments for yourself.

   Along with this, comes a muh lower cost and no minimum investment.

3. A "robo-broker" is a new type of investment broker that has come about in recent years thanks to our technological advances.

   A robo-broker was designed to lower costs associated with investing to make it more accessible.

This kind of broker uses algorithms to advise and make investment decisions about your money.

Before you become skeptical, these investors have shown great success and many people are turning to them these days.

If you choose instead to use the investment plans set up by your employer, you can generally speak to someone in the finance department who can help you set up the auto-withdraw of a percentage of your earnings from each paycheque.

This way, you are investing without even realizing it.

Often, your employer will match an amount of your contributions, which can be thought of as a bonus.

This will help you when it comes to retirement and is very low-risk, if you are risk-averse. Further, you can change your contribution amounts if you get a raise or if you wish to invest a little more aggressively.

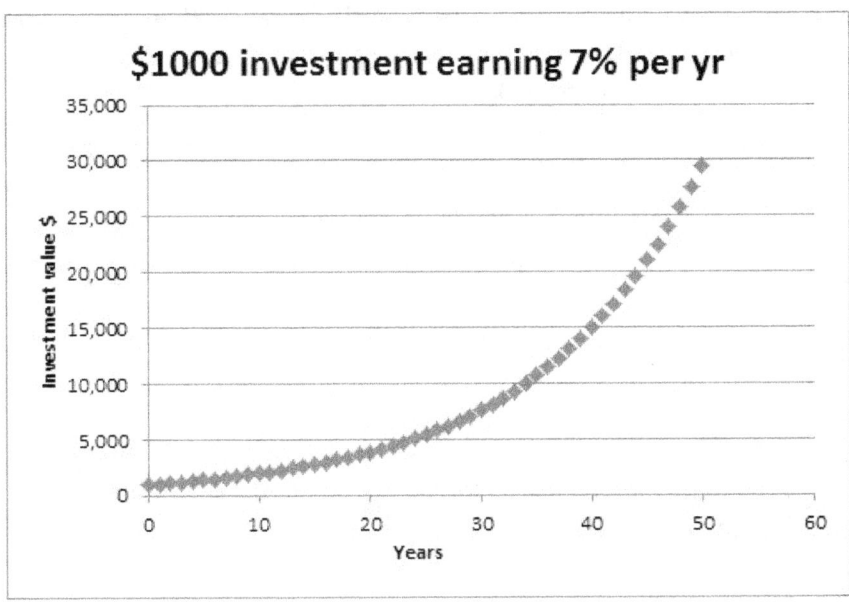

Warren Buffet's Secrets

Warren Buffet is a finance mogul who gained popularity with his investment, business, and finance skills.

He has become a multi-millionaire through investing and business, and people today look to him for inspiration and guidance in these areas.

So, you may be wondering,

what are his secrets?

Warren Buffet uses a school of thought around investing that was created by someone called Benjamin Graham.

He follows the philosophy that the best securities to invest in are lower prices than they should be based on their actual worth.

By investing in these securities, Warren Buffet has been able to get rich! Instead of focusing on the stock market's supply and demand, he examines companies in their entirety, and from there, he decides which companies to invest in.

I mean by looking at a company in its entirety is everything, including its recent performances, profit margins, stock prices, whether they are public, and their debts.

By focusing on the cheap stocks of valuable companies and taking into account their histories and their nuances, he has made large sums of money and has become a pillar in the world of investing.

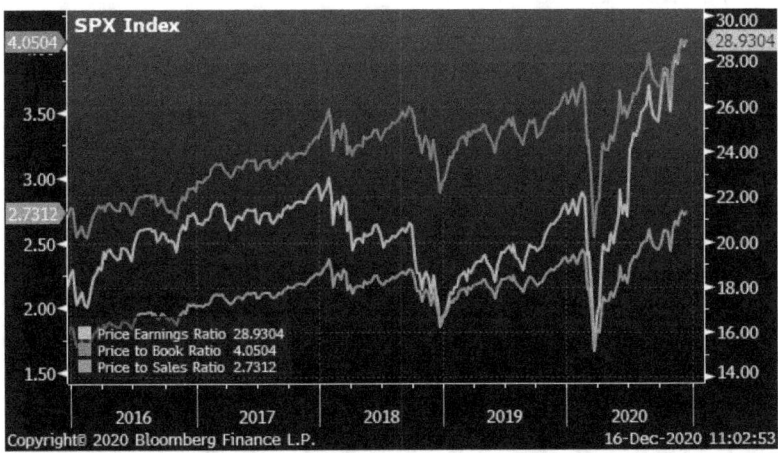

How to Avoid Making Bad Financial Decisions

People with stronger self-control often spend less time thinking about whether or not to indulge in temptations that are bad for their health.

Instead, they can make better decisions for themselves more easily.

They don't let feelings or impulses affect their decision making. They are always able to make level-headed decisions.

Here are ten steps that you can follow to master your self-discipline as it related to your financial management:

Step 1:

Identify your Spending Weaknesses

Everyone has their own set of weaknesses.

These weaknesses could be something like spending money on leisurely activities rather than saving it for future investment.

The first step to addressing your weaknesses is acknowledging your shortcomings, no matter what they might be.

The purpose of acknowledging your weaknesses is not to make yourself feel bad.

Instead it helps you recognize what they are.

Once you are aware of them, you can make a plan for overcoming them.

Once you do this, you will be on your way to investing and growing your hard-earned money!

Step 2:

Build a Financial Plan with Clear Goals

To make investing a successful endeavor, a person must have a clear vision of what goals they are trying to accomplish.

They must also have an understanding of what success means to them.

If a person doesn't know where they're planning to go or what accomplishing their goals would look like, it is easy for them to lose their way or get sidetracked.

For example, one of your goals may be to retire by the age of 55.

Make sure the goals that you are setting have a clear and concise purpose.

For example, don't use goals like "I want to be rich by the next five years."

This goal is too broad for it to have a strong meaning.

Instead, you should make a quantifiable goal, like "I am planning on saving $20,000 by the end of this year".

Then, when you have a quantifiable goal, you can make a plan that makes sense for yourself. In this example, they can plan to save $2,000 every month for the rest of this year to reach their goal of saving $20,000.

They can break down these goals even further and figure out where they can save money or how they can make more money to accomplish that goal in their budget.

Step 3:

Discipline Yourself Every Day

Self-discipline is not something that people are born with; it is something that we must teach ourselves.

Self-discipline is just like any other skill that people may be looking to grow; it requires repetition and daily practice. Changes do not happen overnight; you must work at it for some time.

For example, you may be tempted to take money that you are putting aside in your savings account out for a weekend away with your wife, but you must remind yourself that you are saving for the future.

It will take at least several weeks for a person to see their progress.

Step 4:

Build Simple and Healthy Financial Habits.

To begin investing regularly and retire early, you need to make saving and investing a habit.

This may seem very intimidating at first, especially if you are thinking about early retirement, but you only have five thousand dollars of savings.

To avoid this daunting feeling and keep your eyes focused on your end goal, do the following;

1. Keep it very simple.

2. Break your bigger goal into smaller, more manageable goals.

   For example, instead of "retire early," think about "save twenty percent of my paycheque every two weeks." By doing this, your savings will grow, and you will make a habit of it.

   This will result in early retirement in the long-run.

3. Instead of trying to accomplish one huge goal all at once or to change all of your habits now, focus on doing just one thing consistently and exercise your self-discipline with that one small thing.

For example, if you are looking to start investing within the next year, start by investing a small amount within the next three months.

Instead of trying to invest twenty thousand dollars 11 months from now, which can be very daunting, start with a bite-sized task.

By taking baby steps, you can get your mind used to that habit and slowly increase the amount of money you have invested.

Eventually, once you feel like that goal has become a habit, you can begin to focus on the next goal, like adding new forms of investment or investing the lump sum that you have grown.

Step 5:

Change your Views of Money

Depending on how you grew up, you may have beliefs about money that are hindering you.

For example, you may believe that you "will never have enough money."

This is an example of a money belief that could lead you to make bad financial decisions.

Further, if you believe that "I will never make enough money to retire early," you may spend your money carelessly because you see no point in trying.

These beliefs about money are only a couple of examples of the ways that your beliefs about money could be holding you back and leading you to make bad decisions.

Take time to address these beliefs that you may have and try to confront them.

This way, you can begin to improve your financial decisions.

Step 6:

Create a Financial Backup Plan

There is a very famous technique for handling challenges called "implementation intention." This technique involves giving yourself a plan to follow when you are faced with a potentially difficult situation.

For example; Say a person is trying to save their disposable income to make enough to begin investing.

This person will attend a social event where they know that they will be asked if they want to donate to a charitable cause or purchase drinks and food.

This would normally pose a challenge since they would find it easier to say yes and spend the money than to come up with an excuse as to why they cannot spend their extra money.

Using Implementation Intention, instead of saying "yes" like they normally do, they will come up with a way to politely decline the invitation, so that when faced with the situation, they are prepared.

This way, they will not give in and later regret their bad financial decision.

Step 7:

Reward Yourself When you've Achieved Financial Success

Like anything else in life, it is necessary to give yourself a break and reward yourself. Saving money aggressively for the future, or watching the stock market every morning can be exhausting.

Give yourself something to look forward to by planning an appropriate reward when you accomplish steps on the way to your goals.

This concept is not much different from when you were a little kid, and you got a treat from your parents for showing good behavior.

When a person has something to look forward to, it gives them the extra motivation to succeed. For example, when you reach your goal of saving ten thousand dollars, or when your initial investment grows by twenty percent, reward yourself.

This will encourage you to keep going towards early retirement!

Step 8:

Forgive your Mistakes and Move On.

Even if a person has all the best intentions and the most well-laid plans, sometimes things do not go as planned.

Avoiding failure or mistakes altogether is impossible, and we should not build a mindset around that.

Everyone will have their ups and downs, their successes, and their failures.

The key to overcoming bad choices or unfavorable financial outcomes it to try to acknowledge what caused it, learn from it, and then move on.

You cannot change the past, and dwelling on it will not help you to move forward toward your goal of early retirement.

Take it as a lesson for the future and press on.

Chapter 4: Real Estate Investments

This chapter will expand on our previous discussion of investment options by looking at real estate investments.

The chapter describes every step of the process, so you feel prepared to take on an investment of this scale in your life after reading.

What Are Real Estate Investments?

To begin, I will define real estate investments.

A real estate investment is a purchase made on a property as a way of making money.

This investment could be in the long term or the short term.

A real estate investment could be in the form of a house flip.

A person would invest in a low-condition property, fix it up for as little money as possible, and then sell the property, hoping to make money on their renovation.

Another example would be property purchased that a person will hold onto over time and then sell later, thereby benefitting from the increase in real estate value over time.

This type is a very reliable form of investment.

Examples Of Real Estate Investments

A great way to earn passive income is by collecting rent every month on a property you own.

You can list a room, a house, or an apartment on any rental site, like craigslist, and find a tenant to rent your place monthly for a yearly contract.

This method is a great, hassle-free, and hands-off way to make passive income.

Before we delve into some of the other ways to make money using a property you own, I have a few notes to make on buying property.

A great option for a side gig is running a property rental. This method is a great option for you if you have an extra property or an extra room in your house/apartment.

Rooms and units could be rented from $50 per night to $250 per night, which brings you a weekly income of $150 - $750 if you rent a space in your own home from Friday – Monday.

Various property rentals can earn you passive income, which we will look at below.

Commercial Properties

If you can afford to buy a commercial property, you can rent it out to someone who wants to use the space to run a business.

This kind of property requires more money upfront than a traditional house purchase, but it can provide you with great rewards in the long-run if you can hold onto it and collect rental income.

This kind of property has the potential to provide you with the job of a full-time landlord if you can make enough income from it.

Event Space

Another side gig that is a great source of passive income is to rent out event space.

This way, you collect a fee for people who want to use your space to host events such as parties, weddings, or anything else.

This passive income source can make you a lot of money with very minimal work required on your part.

Vacation Rentals

Vacation rentals are a growing form of side-hustle, especially for people who live in high-rent cities like New York City, San Francisco, or Toronto.

You can make vacation rentals a larger source of your income if you have a spare room in your home or a property that you can fix up to be rented.

Renting out your room/unit on a nightly basis can make you anywhere from $50 - $250 per night. Some people decide to rent a room in their apartment from Friday – Sunday, as most people use the weekend to have a getaway.

This method allows you to maintain your vacation rental property away from your day job while making anywhere from $150/weekend to

$600/weekend. You also have the flexibility of setting your nightly price, so dates with higher demand like Christmas or Spring break can be listed at a higher nightly price.

Instead of paying rent or mortgage to your home while you are away, you can list it as an Airbnb or HomeAway rental for tourists or travelers to rent.

Due to the increasing cost of nearly everything, people nowadays prefer to book an Airbnb compared to a hotel to save money by having the amenities to cook their food and fit more people into one space.

The Benefits Of Real Estate Investments

As I mentioned, investing in a property is a great and secure way to grow your money in the long-term. If you are in a position to buy a property, I strongly suggest it. Even if you are not ready to live in a property that you own, there are numerous ways to turn this into a passive income source for yourself. One way to turn this into passive income is by using it as a rental property. Doing this can bring you rental income or cover your mortgage payments for you.

The second way is by simply investing your money and waiting for your house's value to grow. When this happens, you can sell, and you will make a lump-sum of money that you earned passively.

It can be challenging to make enough money to invest in a property, but any of the side gigs in this book can help you to earn and save passive income that will bring you closer to buying a property.

There are numerous benefits to real estate investments, and to illustrate this, I have provided you with a clear and easy to read the table below.

	Real Estate Investments	Stocks	Bonds	Cash Savings
High Cash Yield	YES	MAYBE	MAYBE	NO
Build up of Equity	YES	YES	NO	NO
Leverage	YES	MAYBE	NO	NO
Hard Asset	YES	NO	NO	NO
Tax Advantage	YES	NO	MAYBE	NO

Compared to other forms of investments, real estate is said to be one of the most reliable and secure.

This kind of investment is great for those who are risk-averse and have the money to invest in a tangible, reliable investment.

Types Of Properties

In this section, I will break down the different types of real estate investment properties.

Rental Properties

As discussed previously, this is one of the most popular forms of real estate investment.

This kind of real estate investment is when a person buys a property intending to hold onto it and rent it out for rental income.

This property could include a condo, a house, an apartment complex, or a building used as an event space.

House Flipping

As I touched on earlier, some people invest in real estate by purchasing a house for little money, fixing it up for as little cost as possible, and quickly selling it at a much higher price than purchasing it.

This kind of real estate investment provides people with quick lump sums of profit, but it requires them to be build-savvy and work quickly, under pressure.

Real Estate Investment Groups

This kind of real estate investment involves a small mutual fund that purchases rental properties.

People can then purchase units or apartments from the company that purchased the entire property.

Once a person has purchased a unit or several units, the company in charge of the property will rent them to tenants.

In this case, the real estate company will take care of all logistics involved in renting a property, from advertising to maintenance and everything in between.

Tips for The Negotiation Process

One very common mistake that beginners make when investing in real estate is being unprepared for the negotiation process.

The negotiation is an important step in the process, and you must know what to expect, and how to react so that you come out of it satisfied.

Below are some tips for the negotiation process.

Win, Win

Keep in mind that you are not trying to "win," you are trying to find a solution that works for everybody; in other words, a win, win.

Negotiate terms, not just price

Remember that not only are you negotiating the price, you are also negotiating the terms of the sale. If they are not willing to budge on price, see if you can adjust the terms.

Remain creative.

Think of new options if you feel like you have reached a standstill in the negotiation. There is no use in giving them an ultimatum, as they will likely shut down. Keep yourself open and be creative.

Make a plan

You must make a plan before going into the negotiation so that you know how to react and what you are willing and are not willing to flex on. Before you respond, remember your plan and react according to it.

It's business.

Don't worry about people getting their feelings hurt or offending them. The negotiation is simply a business discussion. This works the other way too, don't get your feelings hurt over a business matter.

Don't wait for the perfect deal

Don't be afraid to jump on it if the agreement seems like it will work for you. You may never reach your ideal scenario, but if you come close, go for it.

Which Properties Will Be Most Lucrative In the Long-Run?

Below you can see which real estate investment properties are the most lucrative, which will help you choose which type of property you should invest your money into.

Commercial Real Estate

Commercial real estate includes a variety of different commercially available spaces such as;

- *Office space*

- *Industrial space*

- Parking spaces and parking lots

- Retail space

- Restaurant and service industry space

- Etc.

Commercial real estate involves renting to businesses, which is generally a smoother process than renting to individuals for residential purposes.

Further, as a commercial landlord, you can charge much higher prices, especially if your space is in a highly desirable location.

Residential Rental Real Estate

Residential real estate is the second most desirable type of rental property.

This kind of investment involves renting your property monthly to an individual every month, collecting rent, and acting as the landlord.

This kind of rental can offer high income, as the tenants can pay your mortgage while your property value increases.

Properties For Flipping

The third most lucrative kind of real estate investment is the "fixer-upper" or the house flipping type of investment.

This kind of investment can provide you with quick income.

Still, it relies on your ability to work quickly and efficiently and your ability to fix up and renovate the property according to code and potential buyer's preferences.

How To Find The Best Investment Properties

There are different avenues to take when you are looking for investment properties.

The avenue that you choose will depend on the type of property that you are looking for.

Below, we will look at the different options available to you.

Using a Real-Estate Agent

If you are using a real estate agent to find your properties, it will cost you, but the cost comes with numerous benefits.

Firstly, you will have access to the newest listings, as real estate agents use a computer system that includes the newest listings as they are posted.

You will also have someone to schedule your viewings and communicate with the agents that are listing the properties.

Another benefit of using an agent is that they will help you to negotiate and come out with your desired price at the end of the sale.

In addition to this, if you are looking for commercial property or rental space, you may need to use a realtor to help you find available properties since they may not be readily available on the most common property listing platforms.

There are realtors who specialize in certain types of real estate who can help you if you are new to commercial real estate.

Buying on your Own

There are also benefits to buying properties without using an agent.

If you can find the property you desire and close the sale on your own, you will save money.

This fact is especially the case if you are looking for a residential property.

If you have experience in the real estate world, you may be confident enough to negotiate, and you may know what questions to ask before buying.

If you are not but you have a close relative who is, this could benefit you by saving you the commission fee of using a realtor.

Judicial Auctions

A judicial auction is an auction that sells off properties at very low prices.

The houses sold in these auctions are bought sight unseen, but the discount you get on them makes it worthwhile.

There are many benefits to buying a property in this way.

Firstly, you are earning money when you buy, since you are buying at such a discounted price.

Even if the house in in rough shape, you are buying at a lower price than the worth of the house, meaning that you are making money immediately.

Finding Discounted Properties

Our discussion of judicial auctions brings me to another point, which is discounted houses.

You already know that you can purchase discounted houses in this way, but there are other methods as well.

For example, you can find discounted houses when people must sell in a hurry.

This could be for a number of reasons, such as a divorce, a change in jobs or any other reason that means a person has to leave the area in a hurry.

The good thing about finding properties in this way is that they are looking to sell quickly, so they are likely not too concerned about the amount that the property sells for.

This is a great opportunity for reselling, or for renovating to sell at a much higher price than you bought for.

How To Finance Your Property

It can be challenging to make enough money to invest in a property, but any of the side gigs in this book can help you to earn and save passive income that will bring you closer to buying a property.

For example, if you had enough money for a down payment for a property, think $50,000 - $100,000 at least, then you could invest in a home and turn it into a property where it generates rental income for you.

Let's say you got a decent mortgage from your local bank, and you put down a $50,000 down payment for a $300,000 home.

Now let's say you agreed to a monthly payment of $2,500 to your bank plus a 2.5% interest rate for ten years, which leads you to pay around $2560 a month.

Since property prices tend to increase with time depending on where you live naturally, it's safe to say that your $300,000 investment could become a $400,000 investment in a few years.

If you rent out your new property to tenants that cover the full mortgage ($2560), this means that you are no longer making payments to the bank, the tenants are, and you get to keep your money growing on your property.

By spending $50,000 on your down payment, you are generating over $300,000 of income over the next few years with a high likelihood of it becoming a property that is worth way more than $300k in a few years.

Let's say in 5 years, your property value has increased to $450,000.

By doing nothing at all, you have paid off $125,000 ($2500 per month x 5 years), and the value of your house has grown by $150,000.

Therefore, in just five years, with minimal work, you have made $275,000.

For some people, that is a decent salary of $55,000 a year for five years. All of this was made by simply having enough resources to build a strong passive income stream.

Rent or Sell?

When investing in real estate, it can be quite tricky to decide whether to rent or sell your new property.

In this section, I will break it down to make the decision a little clearer for you.

There is no right answer, only two options.

You must choose the option that makes the most sense for you!

- Benefits And Considerations Of Renting

When you are looking into renting your new investment property, there are some things that you must keep in mind.

First, if you rent your property, you will have someone paying the mortgage for you while your house appreciates.

This method can be very beneficial, as you can rent for several years while the house increases in value and then sell and make a lump sum of money!

However, you must keep in mind that there are costs associated with renting your home.

These costs include:

- Interest on your mortgage

- The cost associated with a high mortgage payment (if your rental income does not cover the entire amount)

- Landlord insurance costs

- Maintenance, repair, and upkeep costs while renting

- Condo or property management fees

- Property taxes

- Advertising your property to find a tenant

- Broker costs if using a broker to rent

- Checking credit history or other information on potential tenants

- Accounting fees for tax return purposes

In addition to these costs that may seem to be potential drawbacks to renting your home, there are several benefits to renting in addition to the appreciation of your home's value over time. These benefits include:

- Equity for a down payment on your next home
- Ability to write off costs associated with renting your home to offset taxes for your rental income
- If the market is hot, you can quickly turn around and make a lump sum of money in three years or less.
- Benefits And Considerations Of Selling

  On the other side of this coin is the option to sell your home.

  Like renting, there are also several benefits to selling your home.

  The first benefit is that you do not have to spend the time and energy it takes to rent out your home, which can be quite a time-consuming, stressful endeavor.

One consideration that you may not have known is that if you turn around and sell your house, you will likely find a buyer quite quickly as your home will be on-par with market value, instead of being overvalued like it may be if you rent it first.

Another benefit is that you will not have to pay the costs associated with renting your homes, such as listing them, maintaining them, and any fees that you have to pay, such as condo fees.

Another fee that you will not have to think about is the fee that you may have to pay if you rent your home for more than three years because, after that amount of time, your home will no longer be considered your primary residence, and you will begin being charged taxes on it.

There are also drawbacks to this choice, like losing out on the potential rental income and the potential for your home's drastic appreciation over the next several years.

Other Options Related To Real Estate

In addition to buying and selling actual homes, there is another option that I want to share with you.

This option is something called a REIT or Real Estate Investment Trust.

REIT

(Real Estate Investment Trust)

REIT stands for Real Estate Investment Trust.

A REIT is a type of business which operates, finances or owns real estate that generates income for them. REITs are modeled similarly to the way that mutual funds operate, in that they pool capital from a number of different investors.

This type gives investors dividends because the company can buy various real estate investments, and the investor themselves does not need to buy, finance, or manage any of these properties on their own.

Typical properties in a REIT portfolio include hotels, apartment complexes, healthcare facilities, data centers, or it can include telecommunications such as; fiber cables and cellphone towers.

REITs also require a bit more knowledge in real-estate real estate as some REIT portfolios are a mixed bag of different properties.

I don't recommend REITs for beginner investors as there are many risk factors and areas where you must learn about.

However, many professional investors and traders swear by REITs, so if this is something you'd like to do, please do some heavy research and learn about the REITs in your market before investing any money.

TIPS FOR SUCCESS

Now that you understand a little more about what real estate investment entails and how it can benefit you in numerous ways, I will share some tips for success in this realm of investing.

PLAN AHEAD

When investing, it is important to plan ahead in every sense of the word.

Plan ahead when it comes to your money, your responsibilities, your risks, and your finances.

RESEARCH THE MARKET

Before investing, it is important to research the market to make informed and educated decisions regarding your properties, buying, and selling. Be sure to look at projections for the future.

MAINTAIN ETHICAL INVESTING STANDARDS

While you may get by using illegal or unethical tactics in real estate investing, this will not bring you long-lasting success.

Since you are looking for early retirement, you want a plan that you can follow for years to come, so stay ethical.

FIND A NICHE FOR YOURSELF.

As we discussed in this chapter, there are various real estate niches that you can focus on. Find one for yourself and work up to becoming a boss in that niche.

KEEP YOURSELF UP-TO-DATE ALWAYS.

You must stay up to date when using investing as a main source of your income.

Don't sleep on the current statistics, market trends, or any other world events. Keep yourself informed.

KNOW THE RISKS YOU ARE TAKING

As with any type of investing, you must know and evaluate the risks at each step of the way. Ensure that you know what risks you are taking before you take them.

HIRE A TEAM OF PROFESSIONALS

You don't have to be an expert in every part of the real estate investment process. You will thank yourself later.

On that note, don't be afraid to hire an entire team of professionals to help you at every step of the process.

It will cost you some money, but it will pay off in the long run if things are done the right way and in a timely manner.

FIND A MENTOR

A Real Estate Mentor is someone vho offers you advice when needed and who will coach and guide you on the path to successful real estate investing.

Chapter 5: Financial Tips For Success

Now that you have a solid foundation of investing and the options available to you, we will spend some time looking at financial tips to have the best chances of success!

Things to Keep in Mind When Starting Your Own Business

Although this part of starting up your side hustle may seem boring, it is extremely crucial as not doing some of these steps can lead to legal trouble down the road.

We all know how time-consuming and expensive that is, so let's avoid this by being prepared.

Here are a few items you need to prepare for depending on what kind of passive income source you have chosen and what location you will be running your new business (if this is what you have chosen).

Is your business name legal?

Before you start building your side hustle business website and begin its marketing, make sure that another business doesn't already purchase the name you have chosen.

Depending on what country you live in, there should be a free online search where you can look up all registered business names.

It will then tell you whether your business name has already been taken in your residence area.

Make sure to do this step before you invest any money into the business name you've come up with.

Register a DBA or Fictitious Business Name

If your side hustle business uses a different name from your legal name, then you must register for a DBA (doing business as) to use for filing for all paperwork purposes. For example, your name is Mike Smith, and your business name is "Beautiful Properties."

This requirement is normal practice for businesses in the U.S. but may vary from country to country.

Make sure you look into your country's requirements and have it completed to avoid any government penalties.

Incorporate Your Business

& Get A Tax ID

Incorporating your business may vary for you, depending on which country you are from.

This requirement is important for all tax purposes, and different business structures have different ways of filing/doing taxes.

If you don't do this, you will likely operate your business illegally and face numerous fines.

Once you decide which business structure you want to go with for your side hustle business, you need to register for a tax I.D. number.

This number will function as your business's identification with the government.

This number will allow the government to audit/track your business transactions.

Failure to do this may lead to fines and jail time for evading taxes.

Educate Yourself On Employee Laws

Depending on whether you want to grow your side hustle business into a firm or not, you must educate yourself on employment laws.

If you hire someone to work for your business, you must understand your obligations for taxes, payroll, unemployment insurance, wage & hour requirements, workers' compensation, and anti-discrimination laws. Moreover, you can also hire contractors to avoid some of these liabilities, but you would need to educate yourself on those laws. Make sure you get a good understanding before bringing someone else on board to avoid any lawsuits.

Obtain the Necessary Business Permits and Licenses

Depending on where you live globally, your side hustle business may require you to get a permit or a license before it can legally operate.

There are many different types of coaching licenses – make sure you educate yourself on which one you need depending on your specialization and your country of residence.

You should also look into whether you need a special permit to run your side hustle business.

Most countries do not require this, but it's better to be safe than to have your business shut down for illegal practices.

File For Trademark Protection

Although you are not legally required to trademark your business, you can avoid future headaches by trademarking your business name to avoid anybody using your brand for their benefit.

This filing may not be necessary if you are just starting your side hustle business, but as it becomes more successful and well-known, this is a step that you should remember to do to protect yourself and your business.

Open A Business Bank Account

Opening a business bank account for your side hustle business will not only help you separate your personal finances from your business ones, but it will also help you build business credit so you can take out loans in the future as needed.

Go to your local bank and find the best business banking account deal and make use of their offerings.

They usually can offer a business banking account with deals or business credit cards that help you collect points.

How to Be a Competent Money Manager

With all your new knowledge in financial intelligence, discipline training, goal setting, habit building, mindset development, and side gig/entrepreneur ideas, it is time to learn how to manage the extra money you'll save and make.

This section will briefly walk you through what a good money manager looks like and the basics of money management.

Good money managers always share the same three characteristics.

Firstly, they never spend beyond their means, ever. Even if there was a significant opportunity, they would never take out more money than they have to invest in it.

Secondly, they always have a good stash of emergency savings. This location is where they have money saved up for a rainy day, so they don't have to go into debt or bankruptcy.

Thirdly, good money managers assess their risks before taking one. Doing this does not mean they don't take any risks because, as an entrepreneur, you have to take risks.

However, they take calculated risks. Let's cover the first characteristic first.

Good Money Managers Will Never Spend Beyond Their Means

Good money managers will never spend more than what they already have.

What does this mean?

It means that they will never spend more money than they have in their immediate accounts.

Most good money managers will have some savings reserved for emergency purposes.

That stash of money does not get touched unless it is for emergencies.

They also will never take out a loan or pay for things with a credit card if they don't already have that existing money in their debit accounts. Not spending beyond your means will prevent you from getting yourself into debt.

Moreover, most people that spend beyond their means usually spend their money on non-essential things.

They may be tempted to buy a new car as a big sale at a local dealership is temping them due to low monthly rates.

Good money managers will not spend their money on a new car unless it is utterly essential for their living.

Further, they must be 100% sure they can pay off the car without needing to sign up for ridiculously high-interest rates or long financing terms.

Good Money Managers Always Have Emergency Savings

Emergencies happen to everyone.

It can come in the form of a flooded basement or a large medical bill.

Good money managers are people that avoid living paycheck to paycheck.

Instead, they make an effort to save at least 10% of their income every month into their emergency savings.

The purpose of emergency savings is to prevent unforeseen circumstances from bankrupting you.

Those who live paycheck to paycheck without any sort of emergency savings can be thrown into financial turmoil if they are suddenly stuck with a $5,000 medical bill.

As a rule of thumb, aim to have $10,000 of emergency savings that you can dip into if an expensive accident happens.

This cushion will prevent you from needing to stress or needing to take out a high-interest loan to pay for the emergency.

Good Money Managers Take Calculated Risks

Good money managers only take calculated risks.

You often hear of people purchasing and selling stocks to make a lot of money quickly. Although this does work, there is a ton of risk involved.

Good money managers usually would not take risks such as purchasing stock as there is no guaranteed return.

Instead, they usually use their money to invest in other financial products that have less risk.

For instance, a common investment that good money managers like to invest in is real estate.

Although you require quite a hefty initial sum of money, its return is usually quite high.

Here is an example. Kate has savings of $30,000 and is looking for an investment.

She is deciding between investing her $30,000 into several different types of stocks or using her $30,000 as a down payment for a house.

If Kate were a good money manager, the choice she would make would be to invest $30,000 in a house as long as the real estate in her market is steady.

Usually, house prices increase by 5% - 10% every year, which guarantees her an investment return of 5% - 10%.

If she chooses to invest her $30,000 into stocks, she is putting her money at a lot of risks as stocks can drop in price in a matter of days while the housing market typically takes longer to drop, and you are provided with much more notice.

By simply looking at these two options, a good money manager will see that investing in real-estate is the safer choice with high returns.

If you are just starting to manage your money, don't dabble with stocks unless you have knowledge and experience first.

Chapter 6: Other Tips For Success

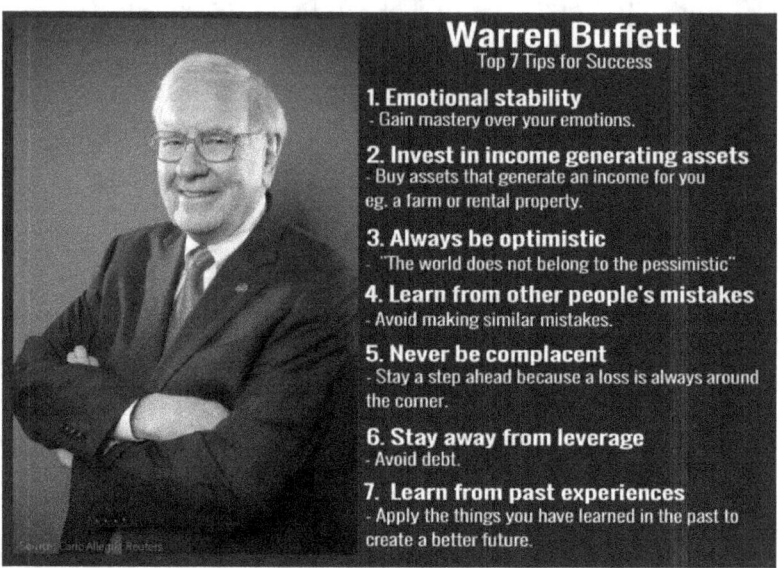

A successful entrepreneur is a person that boasts a high degree of financial literacy, a strong mindset, healthy habits, and self-discipline.

Through reading this book, you have gained the necessary financial literacy to begin making financial choices that will benefit you in the future.

Now that you are equipped with the financial knowledge you need, we will talk about the mindset and the soft skills you need to develop to succeed in investing and being an entrepreneur.

How to Make Investing a Habit

Typically, those who are successful at building sustainable businesses or passive income streams share common habits.

These habits help them live a more well-rounded life that improves their productivity, discipline, and overall drive to find financial independence.

Healthy money habits are not only habits related to how you spend/save your money, they also include the habits that you implement in your overall life that affect how you view your money and the relationship you have with it.

THE IMPORTANCE OF SAVING MONEY

The habits that I will be teaching you will range from incorporating exercise to increasing your perseverance.

Wealthy people face all types of adversity, so having higher energy levels and a stronger mindset will help you overcome the obstacles thrown at you.

Let's take a look:

Work On Time Management

If you are looking to build wealth for yourself, you must maximize your use of time.

Spending most of your time doing things that don't add to your future will only slow down or stop the process of you gaining the success that you want.

To properly build wealth, whether that's by developing and honing a new skill or managing your finances better, you must be able to manage your time properly, so you can put the effort in the right places.

An average person has to work at least 40 hours per week; all hours outside are limited, so time management is crucial.

When people can properly manage their time, they will begin to have room to do the things that matter.

Mainly, they must make room to do the activities they need to achieve the goals they have set.

To achieve their long-term goals, a person must break it down into smaller daily goals that may not be the most urgent but are still very important.

If a person does not have good time management, they likely cannot even get the most urgent things they need to get done in a day, let alone achieve goals that don't require immediate urgency.

To effectively measure if certain things are urgent, non-urgent, important, not important, you need to take a moment to think about whether or not the action that you are doing is not 'urgent but important' or 'not urgent and not important' or 'urgent and important.'

The things that fall into the 'not urgent and not important' category are known as things that are time-wasters.

This category includes things like browsing social media on your phone or binge-watching your favorite Netflix series.

Things that fall into the category of 'not urgent but important' are likely the short-term goals you have set for yourself.

Although they don't need to be urgently completed, they are still important for your self-growth.

Most of the tasks you will be doing to move you closer to becoming a millionaire will fall under this category.

Things that are urgent and important are likely deadlines or any responsibilities that you have to complete for your work.

PERSIST, PERSIST, PERSIST!

When it comes to managing your money and becoming successful, grit and persistence are crucial. No amount of self-discipline would ever be complete without the presence of persistence.

Persistence is a type of habit that helps us to not give up even when we are faced with failure. Persistence helps us get back up on our feet to keep trying even when we do fail

Achieving your goals, like your goal of retiring early, is not an easy thing to do.

It is really hard.

Getting discouraged is easy and something that can happen to anyone along their journey.

This is because the act of giving up requires less energy compared to being gritty and pushing through, even if it's a task that may cause pain in the process.

Successful entrepreneurs did not get to where they are by giving up when faced with hardships.

The hardships you must overcome to achieve your goals are simply something that you have to persevere through.

We have to understand that the most successful people in the world have experienced failure numerous times over and over again.

Failure is simply a part of life, and rather than avoiding it and not pursuing our goals at all in fear of failure, we should learn to persevere and push through even during the hardest of times.

Without failure, we wouldn't be able to reach our goals.

There are various ways that a person can go about instilling perseverance as a habit, but the best and most effective weight is to come up with the reasons you want to do the things in life that you aim for.

If the reasons behind your goals are strong enough, they can motivate you so you can get through anything.

The next time you are faced with an obstacle, rather than falling back onto your automatic bad habits of giving up, try something new and push through it.

Get creative and problem to solve; this will take you closer to achieving the goals you have never before.

Break Down Your Goals Into Smaller Pieces

A good example that a lot of people can relate to is striving to become debt-free.

In our society today, millions of people are crippled by student debt, credit card debt, mortgage loans, and many other types of debt.

If one of your goals is to become debt-free to start saving for a comfortable retirement, you must start building the skills and habits for it.

Those who simply say, "I'm just bad with money!" or "I just love shopping too much!" are employing a fixed mindset where they make assumptions about themselves regarding their inability to save money.

Throw that mindset away and turn it into a growth mindset.

Change negative phrases into positive ones such as "I've been bad with money in the past, but I am going to learn to be more responsible with it" or "I love shopping, but from now on I will budget for it instead."

In this example, people must build better spending habits by practicing different actions until it becomes a habit.

They must also proactively create preventative measures that will stop them from spending money needlessly.

For starters, you can break down your big long-term goal into smaller ones.

If you are $50,000 in debt, break it down into paying off $10,000 each year over five years.

Then break it down further; that's $833 per month. Then, break it down ever FURTHER; that's $208 per week.

All of a sudden, saving $208 per week sounds a lot more manageable than saving $50,000.

Next, place preventative measures to avoid temptations that you know you always succumb to.

If you enjoy going out for drinks on a Friday night, invite friends over to have a few drinks at your house instead, so you don't have to pay crazy bar prices.

If you tend to overspend your money, place a limit on your bank card so you can't spend your money needlessly.

If you are an avid online shopper, get rid of your credit card altogether, or have a friend or family member safe-keep it for you.

This habit will reduce the amount you need to use your willpower and leave you with more energy to work on other goals.

Once you get the ball rolling and it's been three consecutive weeks of saving $208, you should be feeling motivated to keep going.

Try to increase that number if you can.

Open a locked saving account to put that $208 in every week, so you can't access that money even if you wanted to.

Or even better, set up an auto-deposit to automatically transfer $208 every week into your savings account, so you don't even have to think about it. Suddenly, your $50,000 goal has turned into one that happens habitually while requiring minimal willpower.

Create a customized plan that fits whatever goal you are looking to reach.

Avoid temptations while practicing your willpower so you can reach your long-term goal and not only dream of it.

Tips For Running a Successful Business

With your new knowledge of the proper mindset and financial understanding, we can take your financial intelligence and entrepreneurship to the next level by learning more tips.

It doesn't matter if you are starting your first business or if you are well into your 20th business – you still want to be successful.

The ability to own a business of your own will provide you with a strong feeling of strength and power.

You are responsible for making all of your decisions, taking your vision, making it real, and building life-long relationships with customers and other people.

Here are thirty more tips related to entrepreneurship for your consumption:

Get gritty and PERSEVERE

One of the first things you learned about in this book is building a habit of perseverance. Grit is perseverance.

Entrepreneurs NEED to have a go-getter attitude, which is the ability to keep working despite all the obstacles and people telling you that you should give up your dream. Successful entrepreneurs are some of the grittiest people in the world. So get gritty.

Challenge yourself in every way possible

As I said, you have to hold yourself accountable as an entrepreneur.

If you want to be successful, you have to keep challenging yourself to reach more goals – no one will tell you to do these things.

Challenges should keep you on your toes.

If you are someone who is always excited for a challenge, keep yourself on your toes and accept all challenges that come your way.

Take calculated risks

Naturally, people are risk-averse.

People don't usually like to take risks unless they have to.

However, a part of being an entrepreneur can take the risks that work for you.

Taking risks is an integral part of this job.

The most successful entrepreneurs in the world understand which risks they should take and which they should stay away from.

Get yourself used to risks and begin to learn the ones that will benefit your business and the ones that won't.

If you take a risk and fail, it's okay – that's all a part of the obstacles that come with entrepreneurship. Learn from your lesson and try again.

Trust yourself

As an entrepreneur, you will have a lot of people doubting you and telling you that you're wasting yourself.

People aren't just going to automatically give their trust to you, so if you don't trust yourself, nobody else will.

Pay attention to your gut feelings and trust your knowledge and experience when making business decisions.

Be confident and show people that you trust yourself as they will be much more likely to take your leadership seriously if you are a confident leader.

With that said, there is also no problem with asking people for assistance at any step of the way.

Having a mentor is a great idea, and you shouldn't feel ashamed to reach out to one for advice.

Learn to trust yourself, and you are already in a great position to be successful.

Reduce fear of failure

Actions are stopped due to fear. As an entrepreneur, you have to overcome feelings of fear and take action quickly when you identify an opportunity or if you're bouncing back from a mistake.

If you are constantly afraid of everything you are faced with, you won't be a successful entrepreneur.

Don't ignore your fear completely, as that can cause big mistakes to happen but use fear as your guide instead.

Use it to judge the risks you are planning to take but don't let it completely cloud you at the same time.

The more you get yourself accustomed to making certain decisions, the less fear you will fear, and the clearer you will be able to think.

Visualize your goals

A visualization is a great tool for you to learn and master new skills. Visualizing your goals will also help you see them in a more tangible and real way. Ensure you are not only visualizing your end goal but also visualizing every step that will take you there. The more accustomed you get to your plan, the easier it will feel in its execution.

Hire great partners

Hiring strong partners may seem obvious, but the reality is everybody needs a little bit of help when accomplishing their dream.

Hire people that not only have good hard skills in the business you're in but someone with good character that you can respect.

If it comes down to choosing between strong hard skills and good character – always choose the good character.

It is always possible to teach people the necessary skills, but the same cannot be said about a person morals and ethics.

Act, don't react

Successful entrepreneurs don't sit around, waiting for the right opportunity to come along; they simply just act.

Ensure that you do not become caught up in all the things you need to think about, like funding or predicting potential failures, but just talking about these things won't do anything.

Take action to mitigate risk and build a plan.

Spend time

There is no such thing as an overnight success, and no entrepreneur has found success in just one night.

You may not see any results in your first week, month, or even year.

It is normal. Successful entrepreneurs have put in thousands of hours with no result until finally, there is. Keep grinding and keep adapting; in no time, you'll become successful.

Plan your finances

We all know that every business starting up requires money – that's just how it works.

One of the biggest mistakes that entrepreneurs make is spending too much of their time looking for investors and not enough time focusing on other areas of their business. Make a plan for your finances but be sure that you are completing other required business tasks simultaneously.

Identify your customer

The main reason for failing start-ups is the lack of a solid customer profile.

Creating a business without a known customer base, the case may be that the customer doesn't exist.

Before you start your business altogether, do research, and find out if there is a customer base for the product/service you are selling.

Then, build your business around this information.

Take complaints as feedback.

One tip that entrepreneurs need to learn is that you need to listen to customer complaints.

This point is pretty much free business advice. Don't get defensive but take a look at their reviews objectively.

This habit will not only help you identify areas in your business that needs improvement, but you will also gain the respect of the customer by acknowledging their complaint.

Exceed customer expectations

Always ensure that your business is not just meeting expectations, exceed expectations every single time.

If you can deliver more than what your customers expect, you will be guaranteed referrals and loyal customers.

Manage your risks

Remember when we talked about risk earlier?

We should always take risks when running our business, but we should not take on every single risk which crosses our path.

Alternatively, manage the risks by learning to walk away from those that aren't worth taking.

Read case studies

Entrepreneurs may be tempted to use their free time and their evenings to consume entertainment, like watching television or movies.

Instead of watching a new Netflix original series, I encourage you to read case studies instead related to entrepreneurship.

The more you know, the more educated you will be when faced with the next business decision.

Self-promote

Many people have a fear of self-promoting as they don't want to come off as an egomaniac. However, if you aren't going to promote your business, nobody else will.

Build a 15-second elevator pitch for yourself, so you are ready anytime a person asks you about the business that you have started. Using this, you can walk them through it quickly and factually.

Define company culture

In our modern-day, company culture is extremely important. With the glaring eyes of the media, companies strive to be better than ever before.

Set a positive culture for your company starting from day one, and you'll attract higher quality employees, partners, and even customers.

Network as much as you can

Networking is a good idea for every working individual, but it is even better for entrepreneurs.

Never stop networking; get out there and meet people as you never know what you might find.

Even if the people you find aren't able to directly help your business, you may be able to meet someone that can offer invaluable insight to you.

Learn and create

If you hope to be successful, you must have the mindset of a person who is willing to learn and to create new things.

The important part of building your own business is your ability to learn new things and execute them.

As we learned earlier in this book, spend time learning new skills beneficial to your business.

Use your spare time to hone your skills rather than binging a new T.V. show.

Deliver, don't sell

Everybody knows that nobody likes to be sold to.

Rather than selling your product/service to your customers, deliver them instead. Offer some sort of free trial that gives them a taste of your product.

Then, whatever you are offering will sell itself.

Take baby steps

Thinking about the largeness of your goal can be very daunting, that's normal and okay.

Starting a business from nothing is a huge task. Like we talked about throughout this book, the fool-proof tactic is to break it down into smaller steps and goals.

Once you have smaller steps, crossing them off one at a time will help you make progress.

Put everything on your calendar.

Put EVERYTHING into your calendar. Whether it's conference calls, meetings, or even a happy hour with your team – put it in.

Once things are on your calendar, there are no excuses for why you can't do it; you have made the time for it.

Schedule in things like exercise, your afternoon snack, and even a 15-minute break – this will help you break up your day to keep you sharp for other tasks.

Exercise frequently

Earlier in this book, we learned that exercise is one of the healthiest habits you can implement in your life. Just because you want to be a successful entrepreneur does not mean you don't have time to work on your physical health.

As mentioned, book time to visit the gym, go for a run, or even just go for a stroll in your neighborhood. Stay physically active at least once a day helps you take care of your mind and body.

Focus

The daily tasks of an entrepreneur can feel disjointed and scattered, which is why it is important to limit the time spent on multitasking.

Many scientific researchers have shown that multitasking is not beneficial, and humans are not meant for it.

Try to focus on just doing one task at a time.

Giving one task 100% of your attention and focus will help you get it done faster and in a higher quality.

Take time off

The toughest thing for an entrepreneur to put into practice is taking time off.

Many people in North America do not do this as often as they should. Although you may not require frequent time to rest, you do need to take some time off.

This time off doesn't have to be a full-blown tropical vacation; make time for a 2 – 3 day break where you can just rest your mind and body in your own home.

Ask questions

Nobody knows everything. Always ask for help and seek advice from your fellow entrepreneurs or mentors, you know. Asking questions will help you learn more about your task at hand. Don't be shy.

Failing is learning

I have mentioned numerous times throughout this book that failure is inevitable. You will fail, and you will need to accept it.

Get used to it, and don't let it faze you.

Pick yourself back up and keep at it.

Get inspired

Entrepreneurs need to get creative to solve problems and make new connections.

To do this, you need to have a source of inspiration. Make time for things that inspire you, whether it's chatting with your mentor, reading a new book, or building something.

Help others

When starting a business, you will be a very busy person, so it may feel as though you don't have any space in your schedule to help others.

However, helping people ignites inspiration and is extremely beneficial.

It feels good to help other people, so find an opportunity to help someone out, and you never know what might come out of it in the future.

How To Keep Yourself On Track To Your Financial Goals

In this section, we will be discussing all the reasons why self-discipline is crucial to a person's financial success.

We will be going through multiple reasons as to why this is true, and I will provide you with a few tips that will help increase your self-discipline overall.

People cannot achieve their financial goals without being disciplined.

People cannot achieve their financial goals without self-discipline, so make sure you supplement your goals with a self-discipline list.

It will help you focus on the tasks and behaviors you need to perform to achieve your goals.

For example, one of your goals is to save $2,000 in 6 months.

Your discipline list will include putting aside at least $350 every month and avoiding spending money on unnecessary things like fancy restaurants or video games.

High self-discipline in this example would be doing everything on that list without any exception.

This idea does not mean that you cannot reward yourself or take a break from working towards your goals; it simply means that you should get the things done on your list before indulging in any rewards.

Use a daily list to track your finances and to monitor unnecessary spending.

Ensure you are using a daily list to keep track of all the things you need to achieve your goals.

Try to use online tools or just a simple notebook that can help you prioritize and organize.

It feels very satisfying to check off items that you've completed, and it will even motivate you to finish other tasks that are on your list just to feel the satisfaction of being able to check off another box.

Make sure your to-do list works hand-in-hand with your discipline list to help yourself stay on track.

A useful tip to keep in mind when you're feeling unmotivated is to start with the easiest item on the list just to get the ball rolling.

Once you complete one easy task, people normally feel more motivated than before; this will help you get started on the rest of your list.

Starting with a harder task May create apprehension about doing it; therefore, start small and work your way up.

Figure out which obstacles are holding you back from success.

Different people have different things that distract them from being able to complete important tasks.

For example, a person that is easily distracted by emails and people in their office might have to close their office door as soon as they get into work to get their tasks done.

They may delay any phone calls or meetings unless they're necessary to complete their own set of responsibilities.

This act holds for people that may be trying to lose weight. If they know that junk food is their weakness, instead of resisting eating junk food in their house, they can simply get rid of all the junk food in their house, so they don't have access to it. You must minimize and remove all temptations of the distractions that affect you the most when reaching your most important goals.

Share your financial goals with other people.

It may be easier for some people to stick with completing a goal when they have made a public commitment.

The thought of failing to reach a goal in front of other people can motivate them to stick with it.

You can also take this one step further and ask those people to hold you accountable as well.

If you aren't sharing your goals with anyone, nobody will know if you have been slacking off from it.

When nobody is there to hold you accountable, you will likely be less motivated to keep doing it since nobody will know if you failed.

Use external sources or motivation as well as internal.

A saying goes, "don't do it for others; do it for yourself."

However, some people find that they are much more disciplined when they know that their impulses, emotions, behaviors, and actions affect other people.

Contrary to popular belief, it's alright to use external sources to help your motivation. Sometimes, motivation coming from external sources is more powerful than internal motivation.

Find the purpose beyond yourself that is important to you to help give you a higher chance of success.

Discipline is created by creating habits.

When something becomes a habit, you no longer need to draw from your will power bank to get yourself to do it.

For example, if your goal was to stop spending money at restaurants for lunch during the workday, get into the habit of making yourself fulfilling meals to prevent yourself from buying food when you're at the office.

You will be able to see the benefits of saving money if you can stick with it.

Once you see the benefit, you will have more motivation to keep doing it, and soon it becomes a habit where it will feel strange not to make your meals.

This way, you will no longer need to draw from your bank of self-control, but instead, meal-prepping will come naturally since it has become a habit of yours.

Stop making excuses.

Don't procrastinate, or wait for tomorrow, do it now. If you fall off the wagon, that's okay. Start over immediately.

Stop telling yourself that something is too hard or there's something that you cannot change.

Don't blame other people for the circumstances that you're in. Making excuses is the Kryptonite of self-discipline.

Achieve a mindset that is more about "I can do this" rather than "I'll do it tomorrow."

Pay Attention To Your Financial Mindset

A common trend in those who are bad at managing money is their mindset towards money.

Typically, if a person has had bad experiences with money, such as poverty, then they may unconsciously build negative associations with money in their mind.

When a person consistently has negative thoughts towards a certain subject or situation, they may develop an 'unhealthy thinking pattern.' This idea is a common belief for people who see money as "the enemy" or people who struggle to grow their wealth.

Success depends on whether or not the person has a growth mindset. A fixed mindset is when a person believes that their intelligence and skills are a fixed trait.

They have what they have, and that's it.

This idea makes the person highly concerned with what skills and intelligence they currently have, and they do not focus on what they can gain.

Therefore, their activities are limited to the capacity that they think they have.

However, those with growth mindsets understand that skills and intelligence can be developed and learned throughout their lives.

This development can be done through education, training, or simply just even passion.

They understand that their brain is a muscle that can be 'worked out' to grow stronger.

Knowing this, you must employ a growth mindset.

Every skill you have and your intelligence can be improved by putting in the effort to do so. Famous public figures of success like Oprah Winfrey, Steve Jobs, and Bill Gates all employed a growth mindset by overcoming every obstacle that got in the way.

Rather than succumbing to defeat, they worked and discovered innovative ways to overcome previous failures and found success in the end.

Think about what mindset you have right now. If you already have a growth mindset, you simply need to continue practicing it while being proactive about avoiding obstacles and overcoming failures.

If you think you are someone with a fixed mindset, change it right now.

Believe me when I tell you that intelligence and skills can be improved upon with time and hard work.

If you don't believe me, just try it.

Pick a random skill; this could be knitting, programming, jogging, or anything that can be learned.

Set goals for yourself and begin learning something new.

If you can take something that you have zero skill in and become proficient in it, you have just proved to yourself that growth mindsets are real and fixed mindsets only hold you back from success.

Conclusion

This book taught you everything from how to create a source of passive income to how to begin investing.

You learned different techniques that successful people like Warren Buffet used to accomplish their goals.

This book was written simply so that everyone, no matter their education or experience level, would benefit from reading it.

One of the most important things to keep in mind after putting this book down is to have an open mind and be ready to take risks.

Keep in mind that the techniques within this book have been thoroughly studied by professionals in the field of investing.

The tips and tricks laid out here are proven to help entrepreneurs like yourself find financial independence and success.

Now that you have learned the foundation of financial and real estate investing, it's time to put this information to practice in your own life.

Remember, investing is the best method for putting money aside while you work your day job and having it grow with you.

In this way, your money works while you work too!

You will get to see the rewards of this in the future, so remain patient and hang on. Investing is a small step you can take to provide yourself and your family with an easier life in the future.

Take these techniques seriously and try to exercise them in your life.

Many people tend just to finish reading a book, but don't begin any of the exercises or build the recommended mindset.

By applying the information you have learned in this book in your daily life, you will start achieving the goals you have set for yourself.

No matter how young or old, how inexperienced or experienced, or what education level you have, you can use the knowledge and experience that you gained reading this book to begin investing financially or in real estate, which will give you the resources you need to obtain financial freedom and retire early!

www.ingramcontent.com/pod-product-compliance
Lightning Source LLC
Chambersburg PA
CBHW071354210526
45465CB00001B/89